# Sharing

## Christmas

# Sharing Christmas

*Edited by*

## DEBORAH RAFFIN

WARNER BOOKS

A Time Warner Company

A DOVE BOOK

*Special thanks to Pan American Airlines*
*for their participation.*

Copyright © 1990 by Dove II.
All rights reserved
Warner Books, Inc., 666 Fifth Avenue, New York, NY 10103

 A Time Warner Company

Printed in the United States of America

First printing: November 1990

10 9 8 7 6 5 4 3 2

**Library of Congress Cataloging-in-Publication Data**

Sharing Christmas / edited by Deborah Raffin.
     p.    cm.
  ISBN  0-446-51550-7
  1. Christmas—United States.  2. United States—Social life and
customs.    I.  Raffin, Deborah.
GT4986.A1S53   1990
394.2 ' 68282 ' 0973—dc20               90-50283
                                         CIP

*Book design by H. Roberts*
*Illustrations by Kathy Barancik*

*T*his book is dedicated to Mother Teresa, who was generous enough to tell me what the purpose of *Sharing Christmas* should be.

"God will provide. God will watch over us if we are in need. Just pass the word... love for the poor... love for the desolate."

—*Mother Teresa*

# $A$cknowledgments

To thank all those who have made this endeavor possible would take more room than the book itself.

To be brief, the following friends, agents, managers, and just plain good people have been invaluable with their time and caring assistance:

Jeanne Viner Bell

Joanna Carson

Jeri Charles

Norman Cousins

James Jolly of ProServ

Jeff Kriendler

Ellen Meyer ·

Taro Meyers

Barry Mishon

Bob Oettinger and Mark Robert of
          Celebrity Outreach

Trudy Marshall Raffin

Pam Martin Sarnoff

Gordon M. Smith

Susan Strauss

Maurice Tuchman

And, of course, Michael Viner. With his awareness of my desire to raise funds for the homeless in America, he helped me shape the concept for this book. A consistently supportive and extremely patient best friend and husband as I wrote, phoned, cornered old friends, new friends and strangers from around the world these past two hectic years.

Thank you, my love.

*Deborah*

*G*rateful acknowledgment is offered to the following for permission to use this material:

Cindy Adams;  Joey Adams;  Steve Allen; Jack Anderson;  Julie Andrews;  Arthur Ashe; John Barry;  Mary Hayley Bell;  David Birney; Earl Blackwell;  Pat Boone;  Helen Gurley Brown; Art Buchwald;  George Burns;  Leo Buscaglia; Kim Carnes;  Keith Carradine;  Johnny Cash; Oleg Cassini;  Charles Champlin;  Carol Higgins Clark;  Mary Higgins Clark;  Gary Collins and Mary Ann Mobley;  Norman Cousins;  Michael Crawford, "From the Phantom, With Love," excerpt reprinted from the *New York Times,* October 12, 1988;  Ruby Dee and Ossie Davis; Dom DeLuise;  Angie Dickinson;  Phyllis Diller; Placido Domingo;  Sandy Duncan;  Roger Ebert; Jill Eikenberry and Michael Tucker;  Malcolm Forbes;  Charlotte Ford;  Eileen Ford;  President Gerald and Mrs. Betty Ford;  Phyllis George and Governor John Brown;  Cynthia Gregory; Charles Grodin;  Deidre Hall;  Mark Hampton; Julie Harris;  Patty Hearst;  Jim Henson and Kermit the Frog, © Henson Associates, Inc. 1990;

Charlton Heston; Jack Higgins; Jill Ireland; Al Jarreau; John H. Johnson; David Hume Kennerly; Coretta Scott King; Perry King; Michael Landon; Angela Lansbury; Robin Leach and Judith Ledford; Jack Lemmon; Kenny Loggins, "On Christmas Morning," by Kenny Loggins, Copyright Milk Money/ASCAP, Air Bear Music/BMI.; Karl Malden; Henry Mancini; Johnny Mathis; Captain Eugene ("Red") McDaniel, USN, Ret.; Ali MacGraw; Rachel McLish; Ed McMahon; Ari Meyers; Sir John Mills; Juliet Mills; Dudley Moore; Roger Moore; Jeff Moss, words and music of "Together at Christmas," © Henson Associates, Inc. and Festival Attractions, Inc. 1986; Richard Nixon; Charles Osgood; Dolly Parton; Dr. Norman Vincent Peale; Suzanne Pleshette; Sidney Poitier; Anthony Quinn; Deborah Raffin; Rex Reed; Lee Remick; Line Renaud; Burt Reynolds; Fred Rogers, Fred Rogers excerpt, © 1990 Family Communications, Inc.; Kenny and Marianne Rogers; Wayne Rogers; Mickey Rooney; Gena Rowlands; Pat Sajak; Steve Sax; Arnold Scaasi; Francesco Scavullo; Captain Walter M. ("Wally") Schirra, Jr.; Paul Scofield; Eric Sevareid; Martin Sheen; Sidney Sheldon; Dinah Shore; Pam Shriver; Ruben Sierra; Gene Siskel; Jaclyn Smith; Liz Smith; Mitch Snyder and Carol Fennelly; Robert Stack; Ringo Starr; Jill St. John; Oliver Stone; Amy Tan; Elizabeth Taylor; Margaret Thatcher; Lea Thompson; Ivana Trump; Debbye Turner; Robert Urich; Robert J. Wagner; Lawrence Welk; Hank Williams, Jr.; Michael Winner; Jonathan Winters; David Wolper; Michael York

# Sharing

# Christmas

# *I*ntroduction

My heartfelt thanks for your contribution in purchasing this book and the graciousness of all those who have kindly lent their names and talent to *Sharing Christmas*.

All of the participants in this book wanted to give something to those less fortunate and at the same time share their holiday with you. I am deeply grateful for their meaningful contributions.

All of my profits from this book will go to endeavors benefitting the homeless in America. I hope your holiday season is filled with love of family and friends and that you may receive the joy of an unexpected kindness, for that is what you have shown to a stranger.

Wishing you an especially happy holiday.

With thanks,

*Deborah*

# Cindy Adams

*I*T'S HOLIDAY TIME. 'TIS THE SEASON FOR secondhand gifts to come out of the closet.

One December I gave my friend Virginia Graham a brooch. A porcelain, painted, beautiful face. Gorgeous. Stunning. Only I didn't want it. So I dusted it, wrapped it, boxed it, and presented it to Virginia. She oohed, she aahed. Never saw anything so creative and stunning in her whole entire life, she said. Crazy about it and me, she said.

Three Christmases later Virginia wanted to give me a present. You don't need to, I said. But I want to, she said. She did. The same creative and stunning thing I'd given her three years earlier.

Then there was the time Morey Amsterdam received a maroon leather poker-chip holder with his name embossed in gilt. Morey doesn't play poker. Morey plays the radio. Also golf. He did the only intelligent thing. He got rid of it. He passed it along.

To me yet. On top of his gilt-embossed name he had imprinted the word *From.* Beneath that he'd stamped the words *to Cindy*. So my gift for that year was a maroon leather poker-chip holder engraved *From Morey Amsterdam to Cindy.*

I have discovered what means the *X* in *Xmas* : "Xchange."

Some friend actually wanted to go into a store and buy my husband a gift. She suggested the usual tie or cuff links. I said he doesn't need those. I said what he needs is socks.

"We want to give him something he doesn't have," she said. "Give us a hint what he can use."

"Socks," I said. "Black socks."

"How about a solid-gold whistle?" she said.

"Socks," I said. "Black socks."

"He doesn't have one, does he?"

"No-o-o-o." True he didn't have one. Also true he wouldn't want one.

"What's he really need?" she asked. "Let's get something he'll remember us by... like, maybe, a Chinese hand-lacquered harmonica."

"Well," I said, anxious to please, "he doesn't actually need a Chinese hand-lacquered harmonica. He'll remember you by it, for sure, but, I mean, how would you know whether or not you need a Chinese hand-lacquered harmonica? However, he mentioned needing socks. Black socks. Size ten and a half."

Disgusted, the woman disappeared only to settle on a rare book. Something, she insisted, our little family wouldn't have two of. We didn't. The title was *Arithmetic and How It Is Practiced in Five Different Countries.* We can now equate parabolas geometrically in Swedish and Hindustani. Who knows when this information will prove invaluable?

I mean, suppose you're on a quiz show and the category is Aramaic Algebra. Because of some farsighted committee, we could win a fortune, you never know.

One Christmas my friend Elaine purchased something novel for our house. Something we positively didn't have. She strolled Fifth Avenue and, ignoring other fine shops, headed for Tiffany's. Inside the hallowed walls, she purposefully passed rows of rings, watches, and gold knickknacks.

Taking the elevator, she exited at the second floor, deliberately traversed the store's length, bypassed thousands of shiny objects, snubbed myriad inviting cases, and marched directly to one lone counter. There she stopped, fingered her selection, ordered it engraved, gift-wrapped, and sent.

We tore open the wrapping, ripped away the tissue, unrolled the felt covering, and there it lay. A sterling silver lemon-meringue-pie cutter.

She was right. We didn't own one. We don't need one. Who wants one? We dislike cakes and despise lemon meringue in particular.

So, if anyone craves a sterling silver lemon-meringue-pie cutter whose initials are *CHA,* married to a *J,* and will swap this for a pair of black socks, size ten and a half, please contact me care of this book.

# Joey Adams

*T*HE LATE MAYOR OF NEW YORK, FIORELLO H. La Guardia, was my "adopted" father. The Little Flower, as he was affectionately called, was always there to guide me in the right direction when I came to a crossroad. When I ran away from City College for a nightclub job or a vaudeville date, it was La Guardia who would kick my fanny and then call the dean to take me back. When I was behind in my studies, he would put aside his congressional duties and work with me on my homework until I was caught up.

I was sixteen years old, full of energy and ambition, and loaded with ham. My first professional engagement in a vaudeville theater almost turned out to be my last. I arrived at the State Theatre in Baltimore with no music, no experience, very little talent, and an overabundance of guts.

I tried to hide my inadequacies with bluff, brashness, and a phony superiority. When my act died, I screamed at the musicians. I cut up everybody from the stagehands to the manager of the theater. I blamed everyone and everything except my act.

When I came offstage after the last show on the third day, I was no longer the flip little guy who was going to kill the people. I ran, sobbing, to my dressing room. I looked in the mirror and saw a frightened little kid with tearstains and smeared makeup. "I'm just a flop, I'm nothing, I'm quitting," I kept telling myself. It was Christmas Eve and there I was all alone in my dressing room, with no friends or family. A failure as a comedian and a failure as a person. I was ready for the window.

I closed my eyes to blot it all out and then I thought of La Guardia's words: "Don't worry about people knowing you. Make yourself worth knowing." That's when I started to pray. I must have sat there for fifteen minutes talking to God. When I opened my eyes, I saw lights blinking on and off. I was looking through my window at a Christmas tree across the street. "That's it," I hollered, "that's it—my prayers are answered."

I dug my hands in my pocket. My palm revealed that I was worth $1.85. "I can do it for that," I muttered.

I quickly put on my street clothes and I ran to everybody backstage, inviting them to my Christmas party. I was no longer the fresh little punk who barked orders at stagehands and insulted musicians. I invited the electricians, the prop men, the musicians, as well as the other acts on the bill. They all thanked me politely and most of them said they would come.

I was happy for the first time since I arrived in Baltimore. I walked into a big supermarket next door to the theater. For a dollar I bought more potato chips, peanuts, pretzels, and popcorn than I could carry. Ten cents went for paper plates.

I rushed back to my room with the stuff and started setting the food out on the mantelpiece and the chairs. There were a dozen paper plates in the carton, and after heaping each one full of popcorn, potato chips, peanuts, and pretzels, I still had enough of these poor man's hors d'oeuvres for another round.

I glanced at my watch: ten-thirty. They should be coming pretty soon. It was eleven-thirty when I looked again and no one had shown up yet. After another fifteen minutes that seemed like fifteen years, I started to pace the floor. By now it was almost midnight. "What am I kidding myself for?" I cried.

Suddenly I sat up. I thought I heard someone knocking at the door. I muffled my sobs and listened. Yes, there was someone knocking. I tried to cover up my sobbing and my voice came out so high only dogs could hear me. "Just a minute."

Hurriedly, I poured some water in the basin and pushed my face into it. While wiping my face with the towel, I nonchalantly opened the door.

A group of people, laden with bundles, stood in the darkened hallway. Before I knew what was happening, my little room was overflowing with hams, turkeys, candies, bottles, gaily wrapped packages, and happy, laughing people. The entire cast was there, and all the people from the theater.

A little man stepped out of the darkness. He was carrying an armful of packages that seemed to touch the sky.

"Merry Christmas, son," said the Little Flower.

# Steve Allen

HEN I WAS ABOUT FOUR YEARS OLD, I spent the good part of a year living with relatives here in Los Angeles, though my home at the time was Chicago. Even after so long a time I recall clearly that when Christmas approached that year, I was quite concerned, as a conditioned Midwesterner, about the fact that there was no snow on the ground in southern California. How, I wondered, could Santa Claus and his reindeer possibly make his home-call deliveries in its absence?

My cousin Frances explained that since Santa and his helpers actually flew through the air and landed on rooftops, they didn't absolutely require snow. That explanation, I suppose, satisfied my fears at the time, but years later the recollection occurred to me again when, in 1954, while hosting the *Tonight* show, I was asked by Bob Thiele, a recording executive, to write some special material for a little Mexican boy named Ricky Vera, who had just attracted a great deal of favorable attention after making several appearances on Hoagy Carmichael's network TV series, which was popular that year. One of the numbers I wrote for Ricky was "How Can Santa Come to Puerto Rico?" As you'll see, the little fellow expressed the same concerns that had occurred to me back in the mid-1920s:

*How can Santa come to Puerto Rico*
*When there isn't any snow in Puerto Rico?*
*How can Santa bring those toys to me*
*When I live by a tropical sea?*

*How can reindeer come to Puerto Rico,*
*Can they land*
*Right on the sand*
*At Puerto Rico?*

*Jingle bells, jingle bells, jingle all the way,*
*How can Santa come to me on Christmas*
*Day?*

# Jack Anderson

**A**S AN INVESTIGATIVE REPORTER ON THE loose, I have always looked for the story behind the official version of events, a rival account of authorized pronouncements, evidence to measure the truth of popular lore. I suppose it was inevitable that one day I would set out, on my own private quest, to investigate the New Testament story.

So it was several years ago that I flew to the Holy Land to probe through the mists of time for evidence that might corroborate the Scriptures.

Most of the New Testament sites are still subject to historical challenge. They were first located by Helena, elderly mother of Constantine, who in the third century became Rome's first Christian emperor. She relied partly on local lore, chiefly on visions. But most scholars agree that her selections, if they don't mark the exact places in Christ's life, are reasonably close.

Historians have concluded that the Christian calendar is wrong, that Christ was probably born seven years earlier than the date from which we now reckon our centuries. This mistake in our calendar is attributed to a monk named Dionysius Exiguus.

Thus, the Star of Bethlehem should have appeared in 7 B.C. A few years ago, scholars deciphered some observations of the ancient School of Astrology at Sippar, Babylon, reporting the conjunction of Saturn and Jupiter within the constellation of Pisces in 7 B.C. The planets moved so close to one another that they appeared from earth to have a rendezvous in space. From the Holy Land, according to mathematical calculations, the conjunctions should have looked like one large, brilliant star.

It is also known that Jewish wise men studied at the Sippar School. These ancient astrologers, according to the rabbinical writer Arbarbanel, believed the Messiah would come when Saturn and Jupiter met in the constellation of Pisces.

It is easy to understand how this celestial event in 7 B.C. might have stirred three wise men to journey from Sippar to Palestine in search of the Christ. The conjunction would have appeared as a single bright star in front of them as they headed south toward Bethlehem. Or, as St. Matthew so vividly relates: "And, lo, the star, which they saw in the east, went before them."

The Roman governor during Jesus' ministry, as every Christian knows, was Pontius Pilate. Pilate would have been overlooked by history, except for the dramatic moments he spent in the life of Jesus. St. John describes one scene in these words: "When Pilate therefore heard that saying, he brought Jesus forth, and sat down in the judgement seat in a place that is called the Pavement, but in the Hebrew, Gabbatha."

The Aramaic word *Gabbatha* means "raised ground." In Jerusalem, archaeologists have discovered a large, flat pavement of nearly three thousand square yards built in the Roman style of

Jesus' time. It is located upon a rocky eminence or "raised ground."

Here it was, almost certainly, that Jesus stood before Pilate while the mob howled. Upon this pavement, too, the cruel scourging took place. Then Pilate delivered Him to be crucified.

After the Crucifixion, the Savior was laid in a great sepulcher that St. Matthew described as a new tomb "hewn out in the rock." Over one thousand graves have been dug up in Jerusalem that can be traced back to this period. All were located in cemeteries or family vaults, except one. Some archaeologists believe this lone tomb may have been the resting place of the crucified Christ.

Among the disciples of Jesus was one Thomas, the man of many doubts. There are still many doubting Thomases in the world today. The Holy Land has yet to yield up all the secrets of its past, but enough has been unearthed to satisfy many that the New Testament is true.

# Julie Andrews

**F**OR THE PAST TWELVE YEARS OR SO Christmas is the time when our entire family tries to get together. It is comforting to know that at least once a year children, grandchildren, grandparents, sometimes even aunts, uncles, nephews, nieces, and assorted friends, all gather under one roof to celebrate and spend time with each other. I cannot recall a recent Christmas that hasn't been filled with laughter, love, incident, anecdotes—we keep albums of Polaroids and other photographs and now have quite a collection. It is a funny, chaotic, crazy time—and involves quite a lot of organization to bring everyone together—but always after the holidays I think—*how lucky* we are, and what wonderful memories we have. And my recipe Soup Francine really comes in handy.

# ❧ *Soup Francine* ❧

Melt a large tablespoon of clarified butter (or margarine or corn oil) in a wide pan.

*Add: 1 diced onion*
*1 medium potato (diced)*
*Vegetables of your choice, cut up in small pieces*
*(If you use a stalk vegetable, dice the whole stalk)*
*Ground pepper*
*Seasonings of your choice*
*(Parsley Patch all-purpose is very good; sometimes a little curry powder helps)*

❧

Leave all the ingredients in the melted butter on low heat and simmer until onions are soft and a light golden color. Stir frequently; it takes about 15 minutes.

Then add stock, chicken or vegetable (a chicken bouillon cube with added boiling water, for example). Bring to a boil, then let simmer for another 15 minutes.

Let cool. Blend in blender; if too thick, add a little more stock, or if soup needs a little more zest, add V8 juice. As it is stored in the fridge, it may thicken, so add V8 juice as the week goes by.

*Note:* Amount of stock used is optional. I cook for a large family, so I use about a quart, but for single people or a couple, a pint should do. Also, if cooking for more people, use 2 potatoes and more vegetables.

# Arthur Ashe

I REMEMBER MY FIRST CHRISTMAS AS A freshman at UCLA. I was alone in Dykstra Residence Hall where students transferred to if they did not go home for Christmas.

I had no money and was too proud to ask for any at all. So I just spent the holidays alone, had my meals in a deserted cafeteria, and felt awful. I remember those lonely days and I think of those who are lonely today. Consequently, ever since, Christmas has had a special meaning for me.

# John Barry

s CHARLES DICKENS WROTE, "HOW many dormant sympathies does Christmastime awaken." The nativity of Christ is perhaps the most joyful of religious festivals, leading as it does to Twelfth Night—The Epiphany—the manifestation of Christ to the gentiles. It offers up, each and every year, the inauguration of a new phase in our lives.

# Mary Hayley Bell

*I* ALWAYS REMEMBER ONE PARTICULAR Christmas, because it was unusual. It was Christmas Eve and I had just finished rehearsals with Seymour Hicks and was sitting on the small wall by the theater. I was feeling on the gloomy side as I realized tomorrow was Christmas Day—my parents were in China, my brother was coming up from his RAF station, and I couldn't imagine what to do with him.

A man stopped in front of me, and looking up, I recognized Reginald Tate, a wonderful actor and friend.

"What's up?" he inquired.

"I was just thinking what the heck I could do about Christmas for my brother in the RAF."

"Listen, Hayley, I will arrange for you to come to my theater."

"How marvelous! Where? I've only got to the gallery so far as it's only two pounds and—"

"No, not the gallery, the Royal Box."

"Reggie, how divine of you, and I'm going to see you in the Brontë play. Thank you, thank you! It's the best!" I flung my arms around his neck.

The next day, Dennis and I waited with shining eyes. We crept into the Royal Box behind the theater manager, noticing the wonderful curtains and little washroom.

To see this wonderful acting and to be so

near, the tears were running down my face—poor Charlotte! Poor Charlotte!

In the interval, we sat on the floor and ate ham and rolls.

The curtain fell for the last time, and with the rest of the audience we stood clapping. Reggie looked toward us in the Royal Box and bowed. We went on clapping furiously. Then suddenly to our astonishment, he started clapping at us.

"Horrors!" I thought. "What to do!"

It became even worse, for the standing audience looking toward the Box started clapping with him!

"Bravo! Bravo!" they shouted at the boy in the Air Force uniform and the small girl beside him.

"What a Christmas. Darling Reggie, I'll never forget it."

"Keep smiling," I said out of the corner of my mouth and in a desperate whisper. "Keep on smiling, they think we're someone else."

# David Birney

**F**OR THE LAST TEN YEARS I HAVE SUNG IN the choir at midnight Mass at St. Mary's Catholic Church on Christmas Eve in Park City, Utah. I am neither a Catholic nor a member of any choir, nor, indeed, of any organized singing group, and yet this Christmas event, by now nearly a ritual, is one of the most joyous and moving experiences of my Christmas season.

It is a small, plain church of clapboard and plaster, a functional altar attended by a single altar boy, several rows of pews separated by a center aisle.

With me are several of my older children (the babies are home, long asleep), another family with whom we are very close, ten or twelve locals who are regular members of the choir, and an equal number of visitors from out of town, or around town, some sober, some not, who happen to be here for the holidays. The choir is led by the former editor of the local paper (let's call him Jerry), a bright and funny man who is usually well fortified before his arrival by several seasonal toasts to the success of the evening, and who directs passionately, if unconventionally. Each selection is begun with a thunderous sotto voce

exhortation to "Hit it!" And this square, stocky
man with the sweaty, fervent face, eyes closed,
does indeed "Hit it!"—his entire body wringing
the rhythm and dynamic of the hymn from the
close and humid air. It is an extraordinary
performance, not at all musical in its aggressive
athleticism; it is comic, ironic, and yet deeply
committed, and, in some final sense, religious.
We would probably follow him
off the balcony if
he asked, and,
indeed, another
sip from the
inevitable flask
might bring him
(and us) to
that point.

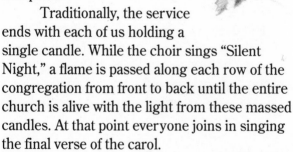

Traditionally, the service
ends with each of us holding a
single candle. While the choir sings "Silent
Night," a flame is passed along each row of the
congregation from front to back until the entire
church is alive with the light from these massed
candles. At that point everyone joins in singing
the final verse of the carol.

As I leave the church, the stars seem still
and serene in the blackest of midnight skies. I am
glad that some of my children have been with me
this night.

# Earl Blackwell

**C**HRISTMAS TO ME HAS ALWAYS MEANT being close to the ones you love. In a small family such as I knew, with two children (my younger sister and myself), we were very close. My father was a soft-spoken Southern gentleman, and my mother was of Italian descent and very emotional, with a heart full of love for us. The Christmas season was always very special.

Upon graduating from college, where I wrote, directed, and conducted both dramatic plays and musicals, I decided I wanted to try Hollywood.

The Great Depression of the 1930s had hit a new low as I set out on my 3,000-mile trip across the country. That first evening in Hollywood, I sat down at the small table/desk in my room at the YMCA and wrote to William Randolph Hearst, the

publishing giant whose two Los Angeles papers I had read from cover to cover after breakfast. Two weeks later, as I was being ushered into the media mogul's private office, Mr. Hearst must have sensed the fact that I was nervous. He smiled and, in a faint voice, asked what I was doing so far from home. I explained that I wanted to be a part of the motion picture industry. After a few more questions, he said, as if to end the interview, that I must meet Louis B. Mayer and that he would arrange it. He did.

Mr. Louis B. Mayer requested a screen test of me, but not until I had lost my Southern accent. Then, Mr. Mayer put his hand on my shoulder and said, "Welcome aboard, you are in good hands." My head was spinning as I left the studio and headed back to Hollywood.

As I walked up Wilcox Avenue and turned onto Hollywood Boulevard, I nearly gasped when I saw that workmen were on ladders taping artificial Christmas trees to every lamppost and hanging enormous red Christmas bells. As I was entering Musso & Frank's restaurant, someone said, "They do this every year and call it Santa Claus Lane." I almost became ill thinking of my first Christmas away from my family and imagining that I was headed for a miserable holiday.

Suddenly, out of the blue, came a wonderful idea! In the *Morning Examiner* I had seen a photo of the University of Georgia football team, taken upon their arrival in Los Angeles to play USC. I telephoned the sports section of the paper to find out where the

Georgia team was staying and was told that they were at the Sunrise Hotel in Pasadena. They would be returning home Sunday afternoon by private railway at three P.M. I decided I would be in Pasadena on Sunday and try to catch a ride back to Georgia with the team, and be home with my loved ones for Christmas.

But suppose my scheme of getting home for Christmas got me reprimanded or even arrested? It took me less than a minute to make up my mind.

I can tell you that when I rang the front doorbell one morning at six-thirty with my heart skipping a beat, it seemed like forever but it was only a moment before my mother appeared, with a wonderful expression of surprise, and then joy, as she fell into my arms. This moment will remain with me forever.

# Pat Boone

I T WAS SHIRLEY'S AND MY SECOND Christmas together as a young married couple—but our first alone, completely on our own in Denton, Texas.

We were married at nineteen, so our first Christmas we were still in Nashville, had both our families' big celebrations to participate in, and felt we'd had a double Christmas! It was wonderful. But then we moved to Denton, Texas, where I enrolled at North Texas State as a sophomore. We were just two young kids with no money, few friends, and each other. We were living in a little three-room, upstairs student apartment. It was going to be a decidedly different kind of Christmas from what we'd ever known.

It turned out to be the most moving, and perhaps the best of all.

Since we had literally no money to spend, we both had to be quite creative. Somewhere we got a little piece of fir, put it on a stand, and stood it on top of a cardboard box in our little front room. Some cotton "snow" covered the box, and we found some little decorations of various types to put on the "tree." But what about presents?

Shirley knew that I had recently done a concert with the Texas Boys Choir in Ft. Worth, and that someone had recorded the concert. She arranged for an acetate recording of the entire performance, wrapped it, and put it under the tree for me. Christmas morning, I was absolutely *delighted* with my keepsake present—and I have it still!

There was a big box under the tree for Shirley, gaily wrapped in borrowed Christmas paper (we *did* have a few friends, after all). Shirley wondered how in this world I had managed to get her anything that big, considering our financial condition. She carefully opened the package and discovered another, smaller one, inside. She opened that one, to find yet a smaller one.

One more time, and she got to the gift. Up till then, it was just boxes and paper, and now she found the pitiful but heartfelt "gift"—a big card that said I LOVE YOU in big letters.

I know it sounds hokey and sentimental, but that Christmas we gave each other ourselves and enjoyed a special sense of the presence and the beauty of the One who started the whole Christmas tradition—by doing just that, giving us Himself.

# Helen Gurley Brown

CHRISTMASES ARE ALL SUPPOSED TO BE wonderful unless you are ill or recently bereaved or something like that. Well, they *aren't!* During my worst—age thirty—I had broken up for the fourteenth time—only this time I *meant* it—with my devastatingly attractive, utterly rotten Don Juan—promptly got the flu and spent Christmas Day with 103° in bed—alone. The actual breakup, three days earlier, had put me in such a state I forgot to deliver a wildly expensive, acquired-after-a-long-search Christmas present to the head of our agency's (Foote, Cone & Belding's) biggest client, the Union Oil Company. When my boss, Don Belding, wondered "why I never heard from Reece Taylor about that present"—it was now six days after Christmas—I came out of my stupor long enough to confess why he hadn't. When

27

we later lost the account, Mr. Belding was convinced the missed Christmas present might have had something to do with it. I think it *might!*

But then Christmas *can* be wonderful. My best was on my honeymoon in 1959 when David brought me to New York from Los Angeles and I got to meet his family, got to the Stork Club, El Morocco, "21," six Broadway shows, Saks Fifth Avenue (Bloomies was nothing then), got to see all those other incredibly decorated New York department-store windows, hang out with writer John O'Hara and David's other beloved pals, all in one week. It even snowed!

# Art Buchwald

**J**EWISH CHILDREN HAVE DIFFICULTY with Christmas, particularly if they live in a non-Jewish neighborhood. I had to deal with this problem. I lived in Hollis, New York, and everybody around me had Christmas trees. It was really a nervous time because we wanted to celebrate Christmas in the worst way, and get the loot that went with it. At the same time, we knew that if we did, we would be damned forever and punished by God Himself.

If Hanukkah was close to Christmas, there was no problem and a Hanukkah gift served the same purpose as a Christmas gift did for my gentile friends. If, on the other hand, Hanukkah was separated by weeks from Christmas, we had to face up to the fact that Christmas morning would be an ordeal for us. It meant going over to our friends' houses and watching them open their packages, and we had to explain that we got so many presents for Hanukkah that there just weren't any left over for Christmas.

Christmas is the longest day of the year for Jewish children, and they have nothing to show for it when it is over.

# George Burns

O NE CHRISTMAS MANY YEARS AGO, Gracie and I had invited our children and all our grandchildren home for Christmas. We had a tree, presents…everything that goes with Christmas, and Gracie had the idea for me to dress up and be Santa Claus.

So, I went to the costumer's and got a red suit, a long, white beard, a special pillow for my stomach, black boots, and a big red hat with a tassel on it. I looked great.

That evening I rang the doorbell, and Gracie opened the door. She pretended to be very surprised and exclaimed, "Kids, look who's here! You know who this is?" And with just one quick look, they said, "Yeah…Grandpa!"

That's the last and only time I played Santa Claus.

# Leo Buscaglia

N AN AGE DOMINATED BY SCIENCE, WITH an emphasis upon the actual and literal, we tend to scoff at dreams and miracles. Christmas encourages and reinforces these parts of our nature. It brings out the spirituality we sense within, conjures up images we know from memories too deeply a part of our universal consciousness to ever fade.

# Kim Carnes

*T*HE CHRISTMAS SPIRIT REALLY BEGINS for me when my family and I drive to the train yard in downtown Los Angeles. The trees are just beginning to be unloaded, Christmas lights are everywhere, there are lots of people, and there is a really festive atmosphere.

We spend hours, of course, to find the perfect tree. After we bring it home, we call our pals to come over and help decorate. We have lots of hot toddies and lots of laughs.

We then stand back every year and decide that "*this* is the most beautiful tree we've ever had."

# Keith Carradine

CHRISTMAS MEANS PEACE AND HOPE. It's family gatherings and children squealing with delight. It's exhausted parents surrendering good-naturedly to the baser aspects of youthful consumerism. It's snowy and cozy and friendly and it smells just like Grandma's house. It's the one day a year when it's acceptable to behave the way we should the other 364.

Photo by Greg Gorman

33

# Johnny Cash

## CHRISTMAS WITH YOU

*T*he times that I've seen Christmas
    come and go are now two score.
*I wish you Merry Christmas and I*
    *wish you many more*
*It's good to see the children laugh with joy the way*
    *they do*
*And it's nice to spend Christmas with you.*

*That ole fashion Christmas is a sweet memory*
*Except for all the Christmases that you weren't there*
    *with me*
*But now I really feel the spirit 'cause I love you like*
    *I do*
*And it's nice to spend Christmas with you.*

*I remember Christmas when I little could afford*
*And I try to remember it's the birth of our Lord*
*And I'll not forget to thank Him for His blessings on*
    *we two*
*And that I can spend Christmas with you.*

*That ole fashion Christmas is a sweet memory*
*Except for all the Christmases that you weren't there*
    *with me*
*But now I really feel the spirit 'cause I love you like*
    *I do*
*And it's nice to spend*
    *Christmas with you.*

# Oleg Cassini

*I* ARRIVED IN NEW YORK IN MID-December 1936 after a difficult, stormy passage from Italy. The city appeared, from a distance at least, to have none of the grace or charm of Rome. I was very scared. I had only $25 when I docked. The immensity of the city gave me pause. Clearly, my arrival had not been a major event in the history of the place.

The next day, I made an appointment with my sponsor, Mr. Ridder, and wandered about the city, mildly disappointed that everyone was not wearing a gray flannel suit and white bucks. Mr. Ridder met me in the most elegant circumstances; he could only assume that I was a young *homme du monde*. He thought my plan to continue as a designer was a good one. "But first, you must travel, see the country," he said. "You must go to California and visit my friends the Basil Rathbones." It occurred to me that Mr. Ridder had a somewhat unrealistic view of my finances.

But then, another thought. He was, after all, my sponsor. Perhaps he was going to advance me the money to travel about the country. He didn't make any offer, but I assumed this was merely an exploratory lunch. I assumed that events would unfold in the continental manner, slowly, politely.

I called Mr. Ridder shortly thereafter. He said resignedly, "I will give you a hundred dollars, which should take care of your hotel bill, and I'll also give you a due bill for another hotel for two weeks. And I will introduce you to the one contact in your field that I have, the vice president of Saks Fifth Avenue. And this is all I will do. The job you'll have to get on your own merit." The hotel he sent me to was the Broadway Towers, a miserable place on the West Side. Mr. Ridder had warned me, too, "Don't even think about looking for a job until after the holidays. No one will see you."

Two weeks passed, and nothing changed. When my due bill at the Broadway Towers elapsed, I had no choice but to check into the YMCA on West Sixty-third Street. They were singing carols in the lobby and serving tea and cookies. I became a devoted caroler, living on tea and cookies for several days.

The ridiculous optimism I'd had about America was now replaced by the darkest pessimism. I seriously considered suicide. I spent New Year's Eve alone in my room at the YMCA while the city swirled around me greeting 1937. Count Cassini of the YMCA. I was just beginning to discern the scorn Americans had for impoverished nobility.

My dejection was complete. I was walking near the Plaza Hotel one day, eyes downward, when I saw some money on the ground. Quite a bit, in fact. I scooped the bills up: $175 in all, a large windfall.

I believed it was a sign from the gods— indeed, it was a turning point of sorts for me. I could eat half decently now and face the world with confidence. The holidays were over, and I proceeded with determination to accomplish my goals as a couturier designer.

# Charles Champlin

T TOOK ME SEVERAL YEARS TO GET USED to Christmas in southern California, with its warmth and its flowers in bloom. Christmas in upstate New York, where I was born and spent my boyhood, was always cold and almost always white.

My childhood coincided with the Depression. The gifts tended toward the utilitarian: the socks and dreaded handkerchiefs and knitted caps and scratchy scarves and underwear, the shirts and sweaters and knickers that would have had to be bought anyway. Dylan Thomas, in "A Child's Christmas in Wales," called them the "Useful Gifts" and waited impatiently for the wonderful, useless gifts.

There were also a lot of hand-me-downs and hand-arounds redefined as gifts in those Depression Christmases, and yet the suspense and the thrills of the season and the great day were greater than they have ever been for me since. I delight in the excitement of my children and now my grandchildren at Christmas, but a little prosperity has made the day an orgy of newness and electrical wonders, which occasionally makes us all wish for less, not more. (We've even taken to drawing names to reduce the volume of gifts, and we make donations to charities in lieu of some of the presents.)

What survives of Christmas is the supreme

sense of family, the gathering in of the clan. The day had always had a particular poignance for me. My father, estranged from us but brought home to his mother's house across the street from ours during his last illness, died on Christmas morning, a gray, cold, and for once snowless day, when I was twelve and my brother eight. It was a long time ago and yet, out of the remembered loss, I feel on Christmas Day an undiminished gratitude for my own family,
extended as
it now is.

# Carol Higgins Clark

**O**NE OF THE BEST MEMORIES OF CHRISTMAS was when I was six years old and my mother gave my brothers and sisters and me ten dollars each to do our shopping. She dropped us off at Valley Fair, our local equivalent of K Mart, and set us loose.

Who's easier to shop for than your grandmothers? They will always love anything you buy them. But that year I put even a grandmother to the ultimate challenge of producing squeals of delight. I bestowed on both of them a 45 rpm record of the "Singing Nun" trilling her hit, "Dominique, nique, nique." I figured it was a good present because they were both religious. It never occurred to me that neither of them owned a record player. Oh, well. They would probably have stopped listening to her anyway. That nun ended up leaving the convent, God forbid.

No matter what presents little children give, adults will find them endearing. But I think the one my five-year-old nephew, Andrew, inadvertently gave my mother last year tops the list. He held up numerical candles we were about to place on her Christmas Eve birthday cake, frowned thoughtfully, and asked, "Is Mimi 26 or 62?"

# Mary Higgins Clark

I N MY GROWING-UP DAYS IN THE BRONX, we always put the Christmas tree in the corner adjacent to the stairwell. That spot seemed perfect for it. The twinkling lights shone through the banister railings. The reflection was caught in the front windows, and for practical purposes, if the tree did not sit properly in the stand—the usual situation—who would notice that the snug corner was offering a little extra support? The exasperating, frustrating, yet joyous task of trimming the tree, testing the bulbs, stringing fasteners through the ornaments, and unraveling the tinsel was always reserved for Christmas Eve. Even though it was a busy time at his Irish pub, my father never failed to rush home for a few hours in the early morning to share the tree-trimming ritual and to help me cut my birthday cake. I, the middle child, was born on Christmas Eve.

Christmas Eve of 1939, my twelfth birthday, was different. The tree, still bound by twine, was propped in the appointed spot, the boxes of ornaments and lights stacked around it. It was not a festive holiday. My father had died in May. Joseph, my thirteen-year-old brother, was on the critical list in the hospital. Osteomyelitis of the hipbone was the diagnosis. Mother was told that only an operation to remove that diseased hip would surely save Joseph's life. That operation would condemn him to a wheelchair.

Sick as he was, Joseph wanted all his presents brought to the hospital. Mother, seven-year-old Johnny, and I made the long three-bus journey, our arms filled with gifts. The most awkward to carry was a hockey stick, the present Joe wanted most. All through that interminable ride, I realized that Mother's eyes never left it. When we arrived at the hospital, she put the hockey stick in Joseph's hands. "You'll use it next year," she promised him. She had decided to take the one-in-a-million chance the doctors had offered. A sulfa drug had been developed. Still highly experimental and with unknown potential side effects, it was the only alternative to the operation. Knowing the risk, she signed the permission slip.

Handsome twenty-year-old Warren Clark, our around-the-corner neighbor, had just returned from college and, hearing about Joseph, hurried to the hospital to register as a blood donor. He drove Mother and Johnny and me home that day and seeing our neglected tree, offered to put it up for us. I helped unravel the strings of lights and handed Warren the ornaments, my eyes shining with hero worship.

Mother won the gamble. The sulfa drugs killed the infection. Joseph recovered, a long, arduous struggle in which he paced back and forth through the house, forcing strength into his muscles, refusing to limp. Two years later he was on the hockey team again, skating with all his old strength and swiftness, twirling me on the ice: "Come on, Mary. Don't be afraid. I won't let you fall."

Christmas 1949. The tree got short shrift that year. We were all too busy with wedding preparations. On the day after Christmas, Warren Clark and I were married.

Now at Christmastime I put up the tree with my children and grandchildren and smile to see some of the battered ornaments that are relics of those early days in the Bronx. I hang the stockings of my grandchildren; four now, soon to be five, and realize it was just yesterday Warren and I were putting up stockings for our own five. I sense the presence of the ones no longer here. Warren. My mother and father. My brothers.

I realize the lifelong lesson I learned on that long-ago Christmas Eve. The happy holidays must be cherished and savored because they may not come again. But the gift of the Christ Child is that the saddest and most difficult holidays may hold the seeds and promise of future joy.

# Gary Collins
## and
# Mary Ann Mobley

### *DUSTY*

CHRISTMAS IS A TIME WHEN THE SUBLIME can tumble into the ridiculous.

When our daughter, Clancy, was five, she saw a television ad for Dusty and her horse. This was prominently listed in her letter to Santa and we heard about Dusty daily. Mary Ann and I could not find Dusty. I located the toy maker in Cincinnati. There was a Dusty, but there had been production problems. Shipment was impossible. But wait! Our friend Jack Booch, a teacher at a university in Ohio, loved Clancy. He would help us. I called him. It was snowing, but he drove to Cincinnati, bought Dusty, and put it on a plane to Los Angeles. Driving home from the airport late Christmas Eve with Dusty at my side, I felt warm all over. Mary Ann and I had the Holy Grail!

We placed Dusty prominently in front of the tree and went to bed secure in the knowledge of our victory. We awoke early and sat near the tree….A noise….Here she comes! Clancy was airborne, clearing Dusty with room to spare. She touched down nimbly with arms outstretched, let go a resounding "Barbie!" and collapsed at the foot of this ubiquitous mannequin in her latest conveyance, the camper. We were reeling!

Dusty didn't matter. Dusty was history. No snow, no plane, no panic. We were getting raves.

Clancy is twenty-one and a senior at Stanford. Dusty is probably collecting dust in a closet somewhere, unused and unneeded, a victim of momentary desire created by a clever television advertisement. Insignificant, yet in a funny way, testimony to the untapped resources within us that can be galvanized when love is the catalyst.

Clancy has said that her childhood was perfect—she wouldn't change a second of it. Neither would her mother and I. You can't ask for much more.

# Norman Cousins

CHRISTMAS AT THE ALBERT SCHWEITZER Hospital in Lambaréné in Gabon, Africa, was the big event of the year. I had the good fortune of witnessing the celebration in 1957. What made the affair so memorable was that the actors were all lepers. Director and producer of the Nativity play was a young nun, Trudi Bochsler, who had been placed in charge of the leper village by Dr. Schweitzer. The village was operated as part of the Schweitzer Hospital, but it had its own grounds about a third of a mile away.

Trudi was clearly excited about the play. Her large gray-blue eyes sparkled as she anticipated the joy the performance would bring to the lepers. I was to learn that nothing was more characteristic of Trudi than her spontaneous enthusiasm and sense of immediacy for things that were worth doing. When she had started to work with the lepers, she went at it as though it would become her life's work. This combination of day-by-day experience and observation and her constant study had now made her one of the best-informed and most competent persons on leprosy in the world.

When Trudi proposed to her lepers that they put on a performance of the Nativity play for the visitors at the hospital, they responded with gleeful anticipation, as she knew they would. Getting up the production for the following day was not an easy undertaking—the costumes had to be located and repaired; the stage props had to be put in order; each person had to brush up on his or her part; and there had to be a complete rehearsal. But Trudi's certainty that the project was well within their reach was shared by all those who had a part in the play.

The next afternoon, I joined the staff members on the walk down to the leper village. The compound in front of the leper clinic had been transformed into an open-air theater. There were several rows of benches, one of which was already filled with visitors from the Catholic mission across the river. Behind the benches were perhaps two dozen young African girls from the mission who had come to pay their respects. They comprised a choir and were to sing during the intermission and at the end of the play.

Within five minutes after the play began, a spell of magic settled over the compound. The singing of the actors was full of life and conviction. Two or three of the leper voices had excellent depth and tone. The costumes were crude, very crude, but they helped to create the necessary illusion. The baby Jesus was beautifully behaved and did not cry until the intermission, and then only briefly. The Three Wise Men were very deliberate in the roles. The leper who took the part of Joseph was compassionate and gentle in his interpretation. Mary obviously relished her role and sang with vigor.

And all the time the play was unfolding, Trudi sat off to one side, her hands clasped and held close to her chest. Her mouth moved in the manner so well-known to prompters.

If I say that the entire experience was almost beyond awareness or comprehension, what do those words suggest? Can they possibly indicate the range of emotions or the stretches of thought produced by watching condemned people give life to a spiritual concept? The play was concerned, essentially, with the triumph of hope through faith; but the brief moment of the lepers in a glittering spiritual universe was surrounded on all sides by the evidence of a closed-in world. Yet in that brief moment, they were connected to the things that meant life for most people.

There was something else. The play, in a sense, was almost a symbol of forgiveness. For the white man in Africa had not, in the main, been a friend. Historically, he had not been a liberator or a benefactor. He had used his superior knowledge and power to capture the Africans and impress them into slavery. He had brought with him venereal disease. He had caused the African women to bear children, and then he had discarded the mothers and their young. He had advertised a religion of mercy and compassion, but there had been little of either in his manner. While I watched the lepers at Trudi's village in the Nativity play, I became conscious of the fact that the play was saying something about a world large enough to hold both black and white. This was close to the original purpose of the play, but original purpose in religion is not too often a remembered part of life. The actors, however, clearly seemed to reflect this original purpose, to which forgiveness belonged.

All this was possible because we were in a segment of Africa where there was a Trudi Bochsler and an Albert Schweitzer.

After the play ended, we sat still for a few minutes. I had no way of knowing whether the same thoughts that had preoccupied my mind were being shared by the others; in any case, the other white visitors sat quietly. Lambaréné, especially at Christmas, became locked in the memory.

We got up to leave. Trudi announced that the leper children had a surprise for us. They had made gifts for each of us—hand-carved letter openers or ship models for the men and beads or pendants or necklaces for the women. Each child had a little presentation speech to make in French and expressed the hope that we had enjoyed the play and that we would come to visit the village again. If the children had also predicted it would be my most memorable Christmas, they would have been correct.

# Michael Crawford

*I* REMEMBER, LATE CHRISTMAS EVE, sitting by the window, watching the planes come into La Guardia over the glorious skyline, thinking of all the people coming to visit their families. I didn't feel lonely. I felt a part of New York.

I'd bought a chicken for Christmas dinner, and vegetables and a really good bottle of red wine. I bought nuts and candies and put them out on the table to make it look as though I were expecting company.

I remember putting the oven on to preheat. "Right," I said to myself, "now I'll do the vegetables." (I often talk to myself. It's a habit, from living alone.) I opened the oven door—expecting that first blast of heat that hits you in the face. Nothing! The oven wasn't on.

I started to take the oven apart (I hope the owners of the apartment are not reading this)—and at four o'clock, I was still trying to cook Christmas chicken. The wine level was now down to a quarter bottle. I put the bird in a tiny toaster oven I found. It came out the size of a fighting pigeon, its legs firmly trussed and in punching position. In its last final fling, after I had cut the string that held its legs together, it shot a plastic bag at me—a second, unsuspected bag of giblets. The chicken had won.

# Ruby Dee
# and
# Ossie Davis

I T WAS SEPTEMBER 15, 1963, WHEN a church was bombed in Birmingham, Alabama. Four little girls were killed. On November 22, John F. Kennedy was murdered.

The sorrow accumulated, and we— including my husband, Ossie Davis, and our friends James Baldwin and John O. Killens— wanted to do something symbolically to celebrate Christmas, which to us really meant to celebrate peace on earth and goodwill toward men. We wanted to overcome our feelings of helplessness.

Our children were six, ten, and twelve then, but they understood what we were doing and why. In our house we decided we would not buy presents that year. We made things with our own hands. The children made things out of wood and paper. I sewed a tie for Ossie. We did the best we could.

Instead of buying a tree, we brought in an old branch that we found in the backyard. We skinned the wood off it and Ossie made a stand. The children decorated it with their old toys and made paper chains that they colored. I remember my son asked, "Momma, will it be all right if we use the lights that we had from last year?"

We lit that branch and it was the nicest Christmas we ever had. We spent our energies raising funds for the families of the children who had died, and the money we would have spent on presents went to them instead. We thought we were giving something, but in truth our family received much more that year than we gave up.

# Dom DeLuise

## HAPPINESS IS A THING CALLED MIKE

**C**HRISTMAS IS AT BEST A BUSY TIME FOR everyone, and even though we try to remember to keep the Christ in Christmas, very often we are overwhelmed with Santa Claus's tinsel and Aunt Sofie's scarf.

One Christmas about fifteen years ago, I was over-Christmased; rushing, shopping, and wrapping when I should've been snoozing, napping, and counting my blessings. In an unguarded moment, Michael, my seven-year-old son, came up to me and asked, "What do you want for Christmas?"

Thoughtlessly and rashly I responded to my impressionable child, "Happiness, and you can't give it to me!"

My wife, Carol, looked to the ceiling and said, "Oh, Dom."

Three hurried days later it was Christmas morning, and I found myself opening a very light present wrapped "oh so carefully" by Michael, who handed it to me with a big smile. I opened the box, and inside I discovered a piece of cardboard upon which Michael had written with a bright red crayon the word *Happiness* in big, bold letters.

Michael said, "See, Dad, I can give you happiness."

Ever since that Christmas, Santa Claus's tinsel and Aunt Sofie's scarf have never gotten in the way of my seeing the Christ in Christmas.

God bless us, everyone.

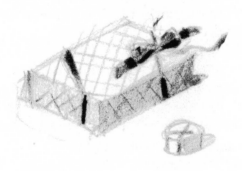

# Angie Dickinson

*I* THOUGHT IT WAS GOING TO BE A VERY morbid Christmas. What I thought was the best time of my life, with the "love of my life," had come to an unexpected end in the fall. You can tell already, this was when I was very young.

I always loved Christmas. But I couldn't stop the crying and feeling sorry for myself. A phone call came from a local popular disc jockey that I listened to a lot myself, so I knew of him. Johnny Grant was once again going to Korea to cheer up the soldiers who were still stuck in Korea and was putting a troupe together. There was nothing like giving totally of yourself to get over torching, according to him.

I accepted the invitation. Not only did I forget about "what's his name," but I saw a distant country, made many new friends within the troupe, and brought joy and warmth and laughs to thousands of GIs. Johnny is still one of my close friends, is vice president at KTLA, and is honorary mayor of Hollywood.

And one of the beauties on the trip was a gorgeous redheaded actress by the name of June Blair, who became June Nelson when she married David Nelson of the Ozzie and Harriet family. To this day, she is one of my very closest friends, and even takes care of my sister, who is in need of constant care. So, she has been a true friend also, is still giving, and I feel that I'd probably never have met either Johnny or June if I'd been sitting by the tree with that "beau" whom I thought I couldn't live without.

So, even though I should not expect so much of Christmas, it is a special time; and it seems inevitable that Christmas seems to want to find us at our best selves. And I keep trying for that. This was one Christmas that I didn't mind giving up my tree for. And the lights in the young men's eyes lit up my Christmas like no others had. The year was 1959.

# Phyllis Diller

*I* LOVE EVERY CHRISTMAS SEASON because everybody speaks to everybody else in a cheery way. People become so open; I wish they'd keep that outgoing attitude the year round. My "Christmas Is" jingle that I wrote continually chimes in my head throughout the season.

### ✳ Christmas Is ✳

*Christmas is cookie time,*
*Christmas is carol time,*
*Candy and mistletoe,*
*Kisses and lights that glow,*
*Christmas is happy time,*
*Christmas is giving time,*
*Friends saying, "Peace on earth,*
*Goodwill toward men."*

# Placido Domingo

**W**ITH A HECTIC SCHEDULE OF PERFORM-
ances around the world, it is difficult
to have my family all in one place at
the same time. However, each year
during Christmas I try to gather us together to
spend a happy and traditional holiday.

Several years ago it had been an especially
busy and exhausting winter as I had just finished
singing a series of *Otello*s at
La Scala. My
family and I had
decided upon the
beautifully
picturesque
town of Hallein,
Austria, just
outside of
Salzburg, because we had
hoped no one would know who
we were. My parents would fly in from Mexico
City to meet us, and we would, I hoped, all spend
Christmas having snowball fights, strolling around
the quaint town, and otherwise enjoying ourselves
like all other families.

However, we barely had time to absorb our
beautiful surroundings when, to my surprise, we
were approached at breakfast by three serious-
looking men in suits. One stepped forward and
introduced himself as the mayor of Hallein and

the other two as town officials. My heart sank as I realized that my anonymity was lost. He explained that Franz Gruber had been the organist in the Hallein church and had there composed the famous carol "Silent Night." He also went on to say that each Christmas Eve celebration, for close to a century, had a special sense of history and pride for the families there. He asked whether I would consider being part of this celebration on Christmas Eve. My first response was "No thank you," since I'd just sung *Otello* only the night before and would not have enough rest as Christmas was only two days away. However, I thought about what the gentleman had asked and eventually agreed.

That Christmas was indeed unforgettable despite the fact that it was absolutely freezing in the church. What a sight it was! The young women and men in the orchestra had to play their instruments with gloves with the fingers cut off, protecting their hands so that they could play. I sang, protected by my coat, hat, and gloves and with steam coming out of my mouth, and everyone in the church sat huddled together shivering. But even while freezing in the pew, I could feel a sense of joy and inner warmth that seemed to transcend the cold. In the end, physical discomfort did not matter at all. A rare sense of peace and togetherness filled us, and we experienced a serenity that is the true meaning of Christmas. I will always remember this Christmas and the three wise men who asked me to sing … maybe not the Three Wise Men, but very wise indeed.

# Sandy Duncan

**M**Y FAMILY, LIKE MOST FAMILIES AT ONE time or another, experienced a lean year or two in the early fifties. I grew up in the oil fields of Texas where one town, Kilgore, was locally renowned for stringing thousands of lights on the thousands of oil derricks clustered in its downtown district. A unique and memorable sight. Those wells are all capped off now, so sadly another tradition has been lost.

I lived in a nearby town called New London; and on our drive back from the annual Derrick/Light Spectacle, Mom and Dad suggested we should hike into the woods and cut our own tree. They made it seem like an intentional adventure rather than a financial hardship.

Finally, we made our selection, and Daddy chopped for what seemed like forever. I think I remember singing carols all the way home and making hot chocolate and popcorn for the tree trimming. That could have been an episode of *Father Knows Best*. At any rate, while decorating the tree, we discovered deep in among the branches a perfect little bird's nest with four small speckled, unhatched eggs. I'm fairly sure I cried for the poor mommy bird. I know my little sister cried. And I know my dad wanted to cry because he got that gruff sound in his voice.

Mom, of course, knew exactly how to care for feelings. She said we'd keep the nest forever and ever and always put it in our Christmas tree with four tiny Christmas balls symbolizing the eggs. And we have. She also said she'd put the four little eggs in some other nest, so they'd hatch. Well, we bought it then, and besides, that's not the point. The point is families have a way of creating warm memories for each other; so what if some are imagined or manufactured. My grandfather, Jeff, and I never bought a houseboat and sailed down the Sabine River either, but I sure loved talking about it, and making the plans and having the memory.

Yeah, sure. I've told my sons the Christmas story, and we put a bird's nest with four tiny Christmas balls in our tree every year.

# Jill Eikenberry and Michael Tucker

**W**HAT WE'D LIKE TO SHARE WITH YOU IS A 150-year-old recipe that makes *the best* cookies. Have the merriest of Christmases.

## ❧ Mary Kate's Christmas Cookies ❧ *(Sand Tarts)*

2 pounds brown sugar
1-1/4 pounds butter
4 or 5 eggs (depending on size)
2 pounds flour (approximately 8 cups sifted)
1 tablespoon vanilla

❧

In a mixer, cream brown sugar and butter together. As you continue to mix, add eggs, slowly add flour, and last, the vanilla. (Recipe can be made in 2 batches, as most mixers cannot handle 2 pounds of flour.) Shape dough into individual 4-inch balls. Wrap them in wax paper and refrigerate overnight (at least). (The longer the dough is refrigerated the easier it is to handle, and it will keep up to one month.)

Place 1 ball on a floured surface and with a cloth-covered rolling pin, roll the dough out flat, turning several times. Get the dough as thin as possible—the secret to these cookies is in their thinness. (The dough should be treated like pie crust—too much rolling or handling will toughen it.)

Use any shape cookie cutter and cut out as many as you can all at once. Take off floured surface with a thin, metal spatula and transfer to a lightly greased cookie sheet. Brush with egg whites and decorate. Bake at 375° for 6 to 8 minutes, or until the edges just begin to brown. Repeat with each ball of dough.

# Malcolm Forbes

**M**Y MOST MEMORABLE CHRISTMAS present was received in 1931. I was probably the only twelve-year-old in America yearning for a mimeograph machine. Since the age of seven, I'd been turning out "newspapers" for home and neighborhood, reproducing them on a tin of gelatin, which would absorb a special purple typewriter ink that enabled you to make a dozen or so copies by pressing a special paper on top of the transfer.

Mimeographing—a word now virtually Xeroxed into extinction—was the foremost way of making inexpensive copies. The A.B. Dick Company's smallest one ($35) included a box of stencils, some lettering guides, and some styluses. It was the depth of the Depression, and I doubted that my father, then struggling to keep *Forbes* magazine alive, could afford to make my great wish come true by stuffing one into Santa's Forbes family bag.

He did, and almost overnight my publishing career ignited.

# Charlotte Ford

*I* COULD ONLY HAVE BEEN ABOUT FOUR years old, and my sister a little younger, but we thought the most exciting thing that happened, then, at Christmastime was to visit the home of our great-grandfather Henry Ford I and his wife, our great-grandmother Clara. The reason it was so exciting was that they had built a house for "Santa's Workshop," and on Christmas evening we would be taken in a horse-drawn sled from the main house to Santa's Workshop, which was filled with toys.

Santa would meet us at the door and, of course, establish first the fact that we had been very good! We were allowed to choose between one and three toys each. The

rest of the toys were then distributed amongst the children of the employees on the estate. They, too, would be brought by the horse-drawn sled and allowed to choose a toy for themselves.

After this wondrous thing, we were then driven back to the main house by the horse-drawn sled. It was like being in fairy-tale land and was so magical.

# Eileen Ford

CHRISTMAS MEANS MANY THINGS TO me. Memories from catching my parents putting my long-desired two-wheeled bicycle under the tree, to pictures of our son Billy throwing up when he saw his first real Christmas presents. It means a year of planning presents, meals, baking, searching for that perfect tree, and seeing the joy of our children's and our grandchildren's faces when they open their presents.

For me, Christmastime means family—a wonderful, warm, loving time that we spend together.

# President Gerald
# and
# Mrs. Betty Ford

**M**AY THERE BE PEACE ON EARTH TO SHINE as brightly as the joy brought to our family this year.

*Betty Ford*
*Jerry Ford*

# Phyllis George and Governor John Brown

*I* HAVE FOND MEMORIES OF CHRISTMAS. Our children, Pamela and Lincoln, both have their own little Christmas plates (one with a little girl and one with a little boy), and they always leave some goodies for Santa Claus by the 400-year-old fireplace in our great room. The goodies had always been cake, cookies, candy bars, and whole milk. Well, one Christmas, Lincoln, who was seven at the time, left Santa some yogurt, a banana, skim milk, and a bran muffin! When John and I questioned him about his choice of "goodies," he replied, "Santa looks like he has gained some weight—I think he needs to watch his cholesterol."

# Cynthia Gregory

OR ME, CHRISTMAS OF 1984 WAS extremely lonely and not very merry. My husband, John, had died suddenly in September of that year, and although I was surrounded by family and friends, my heart was not in it.

Then, in September 1985, certain that I would be alone forever, I was introduced to Hilary Miller. I must admit that it was love at first sight. God works in mysterious ways. After three months, Hilary and I knew that we wanted to be married. On December 28, 1985, three days after Christmas, we became husband and wife. What joy and hope had been in our hearts on that beautiful Christmas!

Two years later we were celebrating the joys and wonders of the Christmas season with our brand-new baby boy, Lloyd Gregory Miller.

To me, Christmas is all about the families. Together with Hilary's daughter, Amanda, and our son, Lloyd, we have our own little family to share the memory of Jesus Christ's birthday.

I thank God every day for being so good to me. I have Christmas with me always.

# Charles Grodin

A S A BOY GROWING UP IN A JEWISH Orthodox family in Pittsburgh, Christmas always made me uneasy. I knew it was to celebrate the birth of Christ, and I'd heard it around that the Jews killed Christ, even though when I saw the movie *The Robe* it seemed the Romans did it. Nevertheless, in my area there wasn't any anti-Roman feeling, just anti-Semitic.

I never heard (if the Jews did kill Christ) why they killed him. I felt sure they certainly wouldn't have done it (if they did it) had they known he was the son of God.

When the Christmas trees all came on in the Christian homes, through the window it looked like a warm, cozy feeling with us killers on the outside.

This has been my feeling most of my life. A few years ago my Jewish wife suggested we get a tree. I was astonished at the idea and told her my reasons. She made a case that the tree wasn't what I said, but more a general celebration of a festive spirit—or something like that. We went back and forth on it for a while, and now much to my amazement we have a tree.

I intend to keep having them, partially in hope that the Christians will drop the killer thing and we will all have a Christmas drink together.

# Deidre Hall

Y THE TIME I WAS ELEVEN YEARS OLD, I was well aware that "Santa Claus" was a myth. I had long since given up asking for all those preposterous, impractical presents. Being one of five children in a middle-income family, it was fairly well understood that practical presents were preferable. Understood by all but my youngest sister. She was undaunted in her desire and determination for a new baby. Not a windup or toy baby, but a real live one. No amount of reason or ridicule could draw her off course. We warned her daily that she was headed for real disappointment.

We all went to bed that Christmas Eve exhausted by our effort to talk some sense into her. Her final act that evening was to place her toy baby carriage in front of the Christmas tree.

At first light we all spilled and stumbled toward the tree, so lost in the selfish greed and grabbing for toys we almost missed the incredible stillness in the corner of the living room. Finally, we followed my parents' gaze toward the drama being played out near us. My sister's eyes, saucer sized, were riveted to the inside of her toy carriage.

The magic of Christmas hit us all full force as we quietly peered over the carriage rim and our eyes fell on the angelic face of my sister's real live Christmas baby.

Santa's sack must indeed have weighed heavy that night. For it was full of socks, skates, sweaters, coloring books, pencil sharpeners, and one little girl's dreams.

# Mark Hampton

**F**OR US, THE MOST DIRECT AND, IN A simple way, enduring method to share Christmas and to be personal at the same time is to make something for a friend or a loved one. As a child, I remember delivering the delicious Christmas cakes and rolls my mother baked for our neighbors. My mother was a wonderful cook. My sister still does this. She is a great cook.

My wife and I have made and painted Christmas tree ornaments for twenty years. We treasure them and love to give them to others. They're personal, they're pretty, and they're homemade. They do not represent money spent.

Our favorite Christmas tradition, though, is the party we have for all the people I've worked with for the past twenty years—the craftsmen and all the people who provide the incredible services for my clients. We have a wonderful piano player, everyone sings and eats and laughs, and the feeling of Christmas camaraderie reminds all of us how grateful we are for each other.

# Julie Harris

THIS IS THE RECIPE FOR EMILY Dickinson's Black Cake, which I used to recite in William Luce's play *The Belle of Amherst.* And since it is a kind of holiday cake, I have given the cakes as Christmas gifts to family and friends, and it has become a tradition in my life. The cake is unique and extraordinary and brings its own Christmas spirit—brandy (not father's best) and all.

My own personal Christmas memory is a picture of my brother, Bill Harris, age one, standing on a horsehair sofa, in his white nightgown with his arms raised above his head and a rapt expression in his eyes. He was asked, "Billy, how big is the Christmas tree?" And Billy threw up his arms, saying, "So big!"

## ❧ *Emily's Black Cake* ❧

1/2 pound sugar
1/2 pound butter (softened)
1/8 pint molasses
5 eggs
1/2 pound all-purpose flour
1/2 teaspoon baking soda
1/2 teaspoon salt
1 teaspoon each cloves, mace, and cinnamon
1/2 nutmeg (freshly ground)
1/8 pint brandy

1 pound raisins
2/3 pound currants
2/3 pound citron

❧

Add sugar gradually to soft butter, blending until light and creamy. Add molasses and eggs (unbeaten). Beat the mixture well.

Sift flour before measuring. Resift with baking soda, salt, cloves, mace, cinnamon, and nutmeg. Beat the sifted ingredients into the butter-and-egg mixture alternately with brandy. Stir in raisins, currants, and citron.

Pour the dough into 2 loaf pans lined with a layer of heavy waxed paper. Bake for 3 to 4 hours at 300°. Place a shallow pan of water on the bottom of the oven. Remove the pan for the last half hour of baking.

Let the loaves cool before removing from pans. Remove waxed paper and store loaves in tins in a cool place.

❧

# Patty Hearst

HERE'S REALLY NOTHING QUITE LIKE
the smell of Christmas: the tree,
the garlands, the turkey, and the
pastries.

One of my most cherished images is that of
the children huddled around the kitchen table
"helping" prepare the Christmas cookies. It's an
annual ritual in our house, like hanging the
stockings and leaving a snack for Santa.

My daughters' special favorites are any
cookies that require decorating! This, however, is
the recipe for one of *my* favorite cookies.

## ❧ *Snowdrops* ❧

Cream 1/2 cup sifted confectioners' sugar
1/2 pound unsalted butter
1 teaspoon vanilla
Add 1/2 cup finely chopped pecans
Measure, then sift 2 cups flour and
1/8 teaspoon salt

❧

Roll into balls. Place on ungreased cookie
sheet. Bake in 300° oven for 25–30 minutes (do
not overcook). Immediately roll in confectioners'
sugar. Place on wax paper to cool. Once cool, dust
lightly with confectioners' sugar.

❧

# Jim Henson and Kermit the Frog

H I-HO, EVERYBODY,
One of the best things about the
holiday season is that you can share
it with your friends. All of the
Muppets work in so many different places:
London, New York, California,
Orlando—the only time we

can all get
together is
Christmas. I
just love sitting
around a fireplace
singing holiday songs
with my friends and family.

Jeff Moss captured
that feeling of friendship in a
wonderful song called "Together at Christmas."
It's one of my favorites, and I would like to share
its lyrics with all of you—along with some photos
from recent Muppet Christmas gatherings.

Happy Holidays,

Kermit
the
Frog

# *Together at Christmas*

## by
## Jeff Moss

*Old friends, new friends*
*Home with the family*
*We'll be together at Christmas*

*Snowflakes, sleigh bells*
*Bringing back memories*
*We'll be together at Christmas*
*Some things change with passing years*
*Let this feeling stay*

*Old friends, new friends*
*Hoping we'll always be*
*Here with each other*
*Together on Christmas Day*

# Charlton Heston

## CHRISTMAS TREE

THE MEMORIES OF MY BOYHOOD ARE thick with trees... Midwestern oak, beech, and maple, but mostly the birch and pine of the Michigan peninsulas. Even in the summer, they dominated the other trees. In the fall, though, the fierce, bright colors of the maples flamed through the woods as the partridge flushed out of the brush ahead of the hunters. But in winter, the days shorten early there and the snow comes soon. The pine turn dark against the white. Driving at night, you could see them black, whipping by in the yellow cone of the headlights cutting through the forest drawing threateningly close on each side of the narrow gravel roads.

The pine woods weren't menacing to me, though. I walked through them to school, played in them and, every December, helped take from them their annual gift to our Christmas: the Tree. There was passionate argument in our small town as to which kind of pine made the best Christmas tree. Blue spruce and balsam were the favorites; our family was firmly loyal to the blue spruce. It's dense, short needled, dark blue-green and lasts the longest if cut and handled properly.

I feel sorry now for people who buy their trees from city tree-lots, packed with stubby fledglings grown for the trade each year. A proper tree is cut from the top eight or ten feet of a mature, forty-foot pine, the top being the newest growth, full of sap to hold the needles longer. Felling such a tree is not boy's work, though I helped trim the branches from the fallen trunk. When this was cut into short logs for burning in the furnace that heated our house, I helped load them on the truck, too. But this was just the Tree's service to our house, not our holiday. The Tree was loaded last, clotted with the deep snow where it had fallen. Then back to the house, the Tree stuck in a snowdrift against the steps as though growing there. Then came a dreary hour or so (*this* was boy's work) throwing the heavy logs from the sawed-up trunk through the cellar window to feed the furnace.

We never put our Tree up until Christmas Eve (Santa's work, as long as you believed in him). Then it was my turn to take part in the sweet deception for my younger brother and sister. Everyone knows the pleasure of transforming a tree into a Christmas wonder, the arguments about how many ornaments, which kind of icicles, the frustration of stringing lights. When I was a boy, we used candles the size of your finger, clipped to the branches in tiny tin cups to catch the wax. These were very dangerous, of course. (So were fireworks, but we all had those, too, on the Fourth.) By God's grace and my parents' care, we never had a fire and the candles were incomparably beautiful, glistening, glimmering among the branches as light bulbs never have since.

I don't need to describe a tree on Christmas morning...we all know that delight. In California now, our Tree still comes from the woods where I was a boy, trucked two thousand miles, not two thousand yards. It's taller now, because our ceiling's higher. But I don't get to go out in the dark, snowy woods on a winter afternoon and watch it fall, crashing in a cloud of snow for Christmas. I can't sit through Christmas afternoon behind the Tree in a window seat hidden from the house, devouring my Christmas books. My first copies of *Treasure Island* AND *Huckleberry Finn* still have some blue-spruce needles scattered in the pages. They smell of Christmas still.

# Jack Higgins

T HE WINTER OF 1947 I WAS EIGHTEEN, A trooper serving in the Royal Horse Guards in the British Army of Occupation in Germany. It was a bad time. Most of the cities were still half destroyed by the wartime bombing campaign. People had to struggle just to exist. We weren't exactly popular. There were many cases of soldiers being attacked while on the town at night. More than one murder took place. Because of this it was common, although illegal, to carry a handgun. Mine was a small Belgian, semiautomatic pistol.

We were stationed in an SS barracks in a small village about twelve miles from a large town called Iserlohn, the nearest place for entertainment. Early on Christmas Eve a friend and I decided to go into town to see a show at the Army theater. We stayed in the bar for a drink afterward and missed the last bus to our barracks. This was not a good thing to do as midnight was our deadline and anything later meant a night in the cells. We stood at the side of the road and it started to snow quite heavily. In those days cigarettes were more valuable than money, and my friend held up a pack of twenty as three or four trucks in a small convoy passed. The driver spoke enough English to tell us that he was passing through our village and accepted the cigarettes in return for a lift.

My friend got in the cab with him and I got

into the rear of the truck. It was filled with boxes, and when I lit my lighter to light a cigarette, I saw the word NAFFI stenciled on each box. This meant they were British Forces canteen supplies, obviously stolen, which indicated that our driver was involved with the black market.

None of my business, I told myself, lit another cigarette, and sat back. We arrived at the village, by now carpeted with snow. My friend jumped out and called to me, but the truck took off so quickly that I couldn't get out in time. I went and hammered on the back of the cab, shouted myself hoarse. Suddenly the truck stopped. I jumped over the tailgate and discovered that the entire small convoy had also stopped.

The men who came toward me looked anything but friendly. They were all wearing old German Army uniforms, with peaked caps right out of a scene in *The Eagle Has Landed.* The man in charge was so angry that he slapped my driver then turned and glared at me. They stood around me in a ring and suddenly things got nasty.

I said, "Look, I'm not interested in what you're doing, just take me back to the village and we'll forget about it."

I spoke a certain amount of German, enough to understand when one of them suggested throwing me over the hedge into the nearest field. I remembered my little Belgian automatic, took it out, and the slider made the usual sharp click that such weapons do when I put a bullet up the spout.

"Just take me to the village," I said again.

There was a long moment, then the leader

nodded, turned, and walked toward a small van without a word. I climbed in beside him, sat there while we drove to the village at breakneck speed, skidding wildly in the snow. We reached the village square without a word being spoken. I got out, and he drove away instantly.

I walked up the hill to the barracks, snow falling, checked my watch, and realized we were already into Christmas Day. As I was crossing the courtyard to the barracks gates, I already knew that I would be arrested, so I tossed the little Belgian automatic that had saved my neck over the wall into a stream that ran alongside.

They unlocked the gate; I went into the guardroom to report. As I was officially overdue, the duty corporal of Horse had me put in a cell for the night. But a savior was at hand, the duty officer on his rounds, who called in at four A.M. to see if anything was happening. When he asked for my story, I missed out on the melodrama, simply saying that I hadn't been able to get out of the truck in time. He told me that I was a young fool, that anything might have happened to me. Little did he know. However, as it was Christmas, he took the lenient view and sent me off to barracks. When I finally got to bed, I had time for only three hours sleep as I'd drawn guard duty for Christmas Day. Strangely enough when I did awake, the events of Christmas Eve seemed like a dream, but it really happened, believe me.

# Jill Ireland

C HRISTMAS WAS A WONDROUS EVENT when I was a child. It seemed to go on for such a long time. Christmas Eve and the excitement of wrapping packages and going to sleep with an empty sock tied to the bedpost. The sound of the grown-ups downstairs, playing cards, laughing, my aunts and uncles, my mother and father.

My mother collected the ingredients for our traditional holiday plum pudding for weeks, and while she mixed it, we all had a stir with the large wooden spoon and made a wish. Daddy worked late Christmas Eve. When he finally came home, it was with exuberance and hellos to my uncle Arthur and auntie Cissy, his wife, and their daughter, Alma.

Christmas Day, awakening to the silence of the morn and reaching out of the snug warmth of the covers to feel my sock with its inevitable orange in the toe, crinkling paper, bags of nuts. And there in the dim morning light across the room on a chair, lumpy packages tied with ribbons, and one year, hung on the wardrobe, a pale-blue organdy party dress with pink satin ribbons. The prettiest dress I'd ever seen. It was like a dream opening my eyes to behold that dress.

Then later in the day playing with new toys in the sitting room while the adults amused themselves at cards once more. The inevitable walk to the cemetery with Auntie Edie to place flowers on my grandmother's grave, my bare knees turning rosy in the frosty winter air. Knee socks, short coat, new shoes, and shiny new hair ribbons, feeling very special, very Christmas Day. Then home again to a big Christmas dinner, always roast beef and plum pudding made by my mother from my grandmother's ancient recipe, written in her handwriting in pencil on yellowing paper.

"Jack's home," my mother would say, delighted. And they would all have a drink. The atmosphere was happy, cheerful, upbeat. Everybody was laughing and kind to each other.

Grown-ups and children alike sat at a long table set with a white linen tablecloth. There were bonbons with crackers inside them set beside each place. We pulled out favors and popped charms and wore paper hats. There were blowers that uncurled with a high piping noise.

I was surrounded by a strong sense of family and occasion.

My friends and I made a tradition of going from house to house caroling, then knocking on doors hoping for a penny or a three-penny bit.

One year when my brother John was two, my mother called after me, "Jill, take John along."

With groans and protests, my friends and I turned back to collect my brother. At one house, owned by a schoolteacher and his wife, we sang our hearts out and knocked at the door. At the same time my brother tugged at my coat.

"I've gone poo poo," he said. The corners of his mouth were turned down.

I knocked at the door again. This house was not forthcoming. There would be no pennies here. Two tears rolled down John's cheeks. With sisterly thoughtfulness I pulled down his knickers, deposited the contents on the red, polished tile doorstep, and beat a hasty retreat to the next house.

"God rest ye merry gentlemen, let nothing you dismay."

We yelled, "Merry Christmas," having left our gift on the doorstep of number 70 Maswell Road.

# Al Jarreau

### CHRISTMAS MEMORIES

Starched, lacy curtains reach into the
night sky
Towers to four year and six year old's eyes
Sills peeling. Pane cracked.
Only books have firesides.
It's no matter to four year and six year old's eyes
Starched, lacy curtains push pull them aside
And pray for good snow
Snow for Santa's sleigh ride.

# John H. Johnson

## THE BEST CHRISTMAS
## I EVER HAD

**C**AN YOU PUT AN ELEVEN-STORY BUILDING under a Christmas tree?

And can you gift wrap faith, hope, and the fulfillment of a family dream?

The answer is yes, if you have the Christmas virtues, faith and hope, and if you never stop believing in dreams that can't be seen.

And the Christmas I remember best, the Christmas that always brings a lump to my throat and tears of joy to my eyes, is the first Christmas I spent in the dream headquarters I built in downtown Chicago.

For me and for my personal family and for the extended family of Johnson Publishing Company, this was more than a mere building, more than a toy. It was, in fact, the first building constructed in downtown Chicago by a Black American, and it reflected the tears and dreams of a lifetime.

All my life, ever since I was a poor, barefooted boy walking in the Mississippi River mud in Arkansas City, Arkansas, I had dreamed of creating such a structure and achieving what was then an impossible dream for a Black American. And my mother, Gertrude Johnson Williams, had sacrificed her life and her dreams to help me make my dreams

89

come true. It was, in fact, the $500 I borrowed on her furniture that made it possible for me to create my publishing empire, and all through the fifties, all through the sixties, when people told me it couldn't be done, she told me, "You can, if you will." And sure enough, at the last moment, when almost every bank in Chicago had turned me down, a chance meeting with a Metropolitan Life Insurance Company executive brought the commitment that made the building possible.

I was determined to celebrate Christmas 1971 in the new building, but there were construction delays. I finally called the contractor and asked if any floors were ready.

"Yes," he said, "five or six."

"Is the water running?" I asked. "If so, I'm moving."

We moved on Monday, December 6, 1971, and celebrated Christmas in the tenth-floor assembly area. My mother, who always made a major spiritual statement at these pre-Christmas get-togethers, was at her best on that day, giving a prayer of joy and blessing that brought tears to our eyes. And looking back on that holiday, I remember not so much the building but the burning pride in her eyes and the fact that my whole family—my wife, Eunice, and my daughter, Linda, and my son, John Harold—was there to share the triumph of the dream. Six years later, my mother died. Ten years later, my son died. And whenever I hear Christmas carols singing in my heart, I give thanks to the spirit for the Christmas gift that made it possible for me to celebrate them in the building, and the building in them.

# David Hume Kennerly

## THE FAMILY TREE

**Y**OU NEVER SAW A CORNER FULL OF Christmas trees in Roseburg, Oregon.

That's where I grew up, and the idea of buying a tree in a town that billed itself as "The Timber Capital of the Nation" never crossed anyone's mind. Some of my fondest memories from childhood were of those chilly days before Christmas when my mom, dad, three sisters, and I would pile into the family wagon and head out to hunt our tree.

We usually ended up about twenty miles away in an area along the North Umpqua River, just past a little town called Glide.

"There's one!" screamed my little sister, Anne. Sure enough, she was pointing to a tree…surrounded by about a thousand others exactly like it.

We drove to the farmhouse nearby, talked to the people there, and sure enough, they said, "Of course!" adding, "Have a merry Christmas." A collective sigh of relief from the backseat. "Do you think we could ride their horse, too?" I asked.

Now all we had to do was select the "perfect" tree. So many trees, so many opinions, and so little time.

In the perverse pecking order of family

decision-making, the choice was little Anne's. This only became apparent, however, following an hour of climbing through brambles, each member of the family marshaling arguments to support his or her favorite, only to be trumped by a single tear coursing down my sister's cheek.

Uh-huh. She wanted the tree she first pointed to, a torn pair of jeans and two sweaters ago.

Then my dad got out the ax, felled the tree, and we four kids hauled it to the car. On the ride home the family sang carols and drank hot chocolate from a thermos.

I'm older now, not necessarily wiser, and a parent, father to Byron, a rambunctious, surprisingly decisive six-year-old boy.

Christmas isn't quite the same here in sunny southern California, where my son is unshakable in his belief that Christmas trees sprout once a year, like giant green tulips, and then only clustered in small lots along Ventura Boulevard.

Then again, some traditions never change.

He always picks the first one he sees.

# Coretta Scott King

### A REVOLUTIONARY
### CHRISTMAS

EARLY TWO MILLENNIA AFTER THE BIRTH of Christ, the earth's two billion Christians continue to struggle with his message of unconditional love and forgiveness.

It is a rare day when I don't find myself wrestling with it. Although I was raised in a church-going family, by the time I got to college I shared with many of my fellow students a fashionable alienation from organized religion and a certain skepticism about the ability of the church to challenge injustice.

I started dating a young ministerial student, Martin Luther King, Jr., who surprised me by saying that he, too, had doubts about the relevance of the church in addressing social problems. But, he added, "to really carry out the precepts of Jesus would be the most revolutionary and dangerous thing in the world."

I remember these words at Christmas as if they were spoken yesterday, for they remind us of the revolutionary nature of Jesus' example and his message. What could be more truly revolutionary than to embrace his militant commitment to love our enemies, to forgive them, to share our wealth with the poor, and to refuse to practice violence?

It is difficult to find this true spirit of Christmas amid the yuletide commercialism and epidemic violence that permeates our communities. Yet, Christmas always brings an elevated spirit of concern for the less fortunate. An added blessing is the decline of the Cold War, which offers new hope for world peace and the possibility of reconciliation and brotherhood.

But the continuing threat of terrorism and its accompanying cycle of retaliation seem to plague the people of all religions. Indeed, history shows that much blood has been shed by self-proclaimed Christians in the narrow pursuit of revenge. Yet forgiveness remains a central tenet of the Christian faith.

Forgiving, whether on the personal, social, or political level, is difficult. But the only alternative to forgiving is unending bitterness, hatred, and a consuming cycle of revenge and retaliation that injures the soul. Forgiveness breaks the chain of retribution and provides spiritual redress for injury.

Despite the war, violence, greed, exploitation, and the unearned suffering of impoverished millions, the love of enemies and the spirit of forgiveness are now more relevant to our survival than ever before.

After nearly twenty centuries, the light of Bethlehem burns as a beacon of hope in the hearts and souls of peace-loving people across the earth. On this Christmas, may we, the people of every race, nation, and religion, learn to love one another, to forgive and be forgiven. When we have mastered this calling, then the peace of Christ will truly prevail.

# Perry King

## A CHRISTMAS GIFT

I T WAS CHRISTMAS WHEN I MET CLAUDE Rains. I was about fifteen, and it had been a harsh year of prep school, endless dreary weather, and loneliness. I wanted to be an actor.

My father had done a wonderful thing when he heard this: he had arranged for me to meet the illustrious but aging English star Claude Rains.

"Who?" I asked.

"Don't you know who I'm talking about? How can you think about becoming an actor if you don't know about the great ones? *Casablanca?*"

"What's *Casablanca?*" (Hell, I was only fifteen.)

My father picked me up and took me away from that accursed school, and after a few hours' drive we arrived at a nice suburban-looking home

not far from Boston. An old man answered the door and spoke to us in a deep baritone.

"Ah, come in, come in. I've been expecting you."

I saw a man far older than my father, withered and worn by life. My impression of him was that he was more than ill—he was near death. I later saw him in many films and realized how little of the physical was left to him. The marvelous shock of hair that had been his trademark was gone, and he stooped sharply. But his eyes were bright, alive with thoughts. There was a look of mischief in them, as if he were planning some practical joke. The contrast between those eyes and the rest of him brought my fifteen-year-old's contemptuous attitude toward adults to a halt. He got my attention—fast.

"Well, boy, I'm told you want to be an actor, and I'm to tell you what it's about. Is that right?"

Imperious words, and a deep baritone voice, but the eyes were shining, laughing at me, and with me. I swear he knew how I felt about adults, and he felt the same way.

"How old are you, boy? Aah…well, I was about your age when I started. It was in London, in…"

—and he began to weave the tale of his life in such a beguiling way that I was taken to London, to the theater, to the stage. I saw his rattling old body start to move as the youth he was describing, and his voice quickened and rose in timbre. He was the first actor I had ever met, and certainly one of the best I have *ever* met. It was the first time I had felt the power of an actor at that range, all directed toward me. He was everything I meant to be. I just didn't know it yet.

"Then Shaw said to me, when he realized what Vivian and I were talking 'bout…"

The stories were incredible, the names those of the gods and heroes of the stage, but I can barely piece them together today. I heard them with the ears of a young boy who had never heard of those names and places before. It was like looking at your destination through a dense fog. But he made it come alive for me—through him I could smell it and taste it, even if I didn't recognize the details. As he began to tell stories of the zenith of his career, I swear he grew in height, and his voice deepened and boomed. He simply *was* where he described and *became* what he described. And then he would cough, or grimace at some pain, and the old man would return.

My father said, "We'd better be going." I didn't want to. I couldn't—not yet. My father nodded gently toward Rains. When I looked, I saw what he saw: an old, frail man, tired and in some pain. The Caesar of a few minutes before, outwitting his Cleopatra, was gone. It was time to go.

I knew so little about acting. I didn't even know what questions to ask. There was so little time and so much to learn. But before we left I said to him, "Sir, what's the most important thing?"

It made him pause, as nothing else had. A good question! He looked at me, almost fiercely, raised a finger toward the ceiling, and told me the most important thing that anybody has ever told me.

"The most important thing," he said, "is enthusiasm."

I can still hear him say it, anytime I want. My mind will play that memory like a tape.

We left then, and that extraordinary man died soon after.

But what a gift that answer was! The best Christmas present I've ever had. I think it's the wisest thing I've ever heard, not just about acting, but about *life*. He said it so that I'd hear it, so that I would take it away with me—and I did. It took me years to really hear it, but since I did, it's been the answer to every question I've ever had.

I wish I could thank Mr. Rains for his gift, but since I can't, I do the next best thing, about once a year. I thank my father—for taking me, on that Christmas so long ago, to the house of the illustrious but aging English star...Claude Rains.

# Michael Landon

## *A Christmas Memory*

OR MANY YEARS CHRISTMAS EVE WAS A time for adults at my house. The children would go to bed after placing the milk and cookies on the hearth for Santa, and the grown-ups would open their gifts and begin to assemble the 7,000-piece dollhouse that's always a piece short.

That all changed a few years ago. My wife became involved with a facility that takes care of battered and abandoned children, wards of the court; children whose pain is heightened at Christmastime by the knowledge that other children are with their families.

We now join these children on Christmas Eve with presents for all and moments of laughter and tears. Our own children join us in this wonderful time and gain a great deal from it.

Being able to share with others has given Christmas a new meaning to my family. Long after the Christmas tree lights have been returned to the storeroom, the faces of these children will continue to burn brightly in our hearts.

# Angela Lansbury

## CHRISTMAS MEMORY

CHRISTMAS FOR ME AS A CHILD WAS A time of cooking. My grandmother would arrive to stay with us for the holidays and immediately start preparations for the Christmas plum pudding and the enormous Christmas fruitcake. We kids looked forward to the lucky "stir," a chance to stir the plum pudding and make a wish.

The pudding had little silver trinkets and three-penny pieces buried in it, and it was considered very lucky if your piece contained one of these treasures.

Two very popular items were individual mince pies and sausage rolls. I serve both of these every Boxing Day (the day after Christmas), and they go like "hotcakes," believe me. I serve them warm. The minced pies with hard sauce or whipped cream and the sausage rolls with mustard.

Hard as I try, I never seem to have enough! I find myself recreating the sights and smells of Christmas for my friends and family that I remember enjoying so much in my childhood.

# 🍂 *Christmas Sausage Rolls* 🍂
## *(4 dozen)*

2 dozen small breakfast pork sausages
2 sheets of Pepperidge Farm prepared puff pastry
1 egg

🍂

Cut sausages in half. Poach gently in boiling water in shallow pan until cooked through. Drain and cool.

Roll out one pastry sheet very thin (16th of an inch) on floured board . With pastry cutter or knife, divide into squares big enough to roll each sausage with a 1/4-inch overlap. Brush inside edges of square with egg to stick. Squeeze ends and mark with tines of fork. When all are assembled on cookie sheet in rows, brush with egg (beaten with a little water). Cut three gashes with knife across top of each roll on diagonal.

Bake in 400° oven 10-15 minutes.

Serve with mustard.

🍂

# Robin Leach
# and
# Judith Ledford

## IT'S A "NEW ENGLAND" COUNTRY CHRISTMAS

CHAMPAGNE AND CAVIAR, OF COURSE, TURN up in my Christmas plans with my longtime girlfriend, Judith Ledford, at our Connecticut lakefront home.

Christmas Day starts off with champagne around the fireplace and the opening of gifts. Then it's traditional Christmas turkey with our special "make-you-sleep" stuffing of Grand Marnier apricot. You're guaranteed a solid sixty minutes of snooze in front of the fire.

Then it's time to begin the biggest cooking extravaganza of our year. In England, the day after Christmas is called Boxing Day—so named for the boxes of gifts or money that the early lords of the manor used to dispense to the servants, and carried on today as tradition for friends.

We cook dozens of Scotch eggs because it's such an English favorite, and our American friends and visitors gobble them down ferociously. Of course there's champagne, caviar, smoked salmon, and lots of other delicacies. It's where the expression "the groaning table" comes from, because our dining room table and kitchen-island counters literally buckle and groan from the weight of the food.

Boxing Day is an all-day affair at our house. Friends have literally traveled from overseas to join in the fun that starts as early as ten A.M. and lasts until midnight. Every year we also remember that there are many people, due to unfortunate circumstances, wholly unable to celebrate the holidays the way we do. So, we always pick two new charities to send contributions to. But our regular every-year donation goes to the City Meals on Wheels project, which provides food for the infirm, disabled, and shut-ins of New York City.

Christmas is the most beautiful time of the year because the Holy Birth sets an example for all of us to bring joy and peace to the world.

# Jack Lemmon

I WAS AN ONLY CHILD, AND I DON'T KNOW if I was spoiled rotten as a kid, but I do know that in my very early years Christmas was the greatest day of the year, mainly because I always got what I wanted. And a lot more.

The Christmas that stands out most vividly in my mind was my seventh. I had asked for two very special presents, both of which I received, and the normal assortment of other goodies. After my parents and I had opened all of our presents, I followed my usual routine—I ran up the street with a huge box full of my presents to show Frankie, one of my pals. Frankie was mighty impressed, as always, but I was not that impressed with what he had received. A couple of nice things, but nothing at all unusual, and it seemed to me certainly less than he usually got at Christmas. And I also kept looking around for a dog, because I knew that is what he had really wanted. And I was afraid to ask him what had happened.

After a while I gathered up my presents and left to go home. Two houses from Frankie's, I passed another friend's house that I had deliberately avoided earlier. I knew his father had lost his job shortly before Christmas, that things were tough, and I guess I wanted to avoid the embarrassment of facing him with all of the goodies that I had been lucky enough to get.

Now here he was, sitting on the lawn in front of his house playing with a puppy. I never saw a happier kid in my life, and he just kept saying, "I can't believe I got him, I can't believe it. Isn't he beautiful?" etc.

It doesn't take a genius to figure where the dog came from, and to my knowledge Frankie never divulged the source.

I know this story sounds corny, but it's absolutely true. And needless to say, it began to teach me what Christmas should really be about.

# Kenny Loggins

### CHRISTMAS IS FOR EVERYONE BITTERSWEET

O N CHRISTMAS MORNING" IS A SONG I wrote with David Foster that expresses a time in my life that I hold dear to me and share with those who have similar experiences.

## ✳ On Christmas Morning ✳

*Old December's here at last*
*A time for celebration*
*Christmas present*
*Christmas past*
    *tumble down together*
    *like the snow*
*What a show*
*Now the snowman*
*Sarah made*
    *is melting by the road-side*
*On the wind a serenade*
    *of children's voices singing*
*"I believe"*
*I believe in us*
*I believe*
*On Christmas morning you*
    *awaken with a smile*
*You hold me in your arms*

106

*We watch the snow-flakes fall*
*And then you love me*
*And I realize*
*How sweet a life can be*
*And all the memories*
   *coming back again this year...*
*On Christmas Morning*

*Sentimental melodies*
   *surround me like an old friend*
*She spent a winter here with me*
*N' silently we watched the seasons change*
*Oh they change so fast*
   *fade away*

*On Christmas Morning you*
   *awaken with a smile*
*You hold me in your arms*
*We watch the snow-flakes*
   *fall*
   *and then you love me*
   *and I realize*
*How sweet a life can be*
   *and Oh the memories*
   *will always take me back*
*Hold me back*
   *in time ... to Christmas Morning*

# Karl Malden

*I* ALWAYS LOVED CHRISTMAS AND I always love Christmas because I celebrate two Christmases—one on December 25, which people celebrate here in America, and like everybody else in America, the family would give a couple of gifts to each other. But on January 7, practically two weeks later, is a Christmas I could never forget because the Serbian Orthodox Church celebrated the old calendar, which meant that I as a child didn't have to go to school. That was a day off from school! The table was laden with food, no gifts were exchanged, but then all the Serbian people would go from home to home eating, drinking, and singing Serbian Christmas carols. So all the Serbian children in my hometown felt lucky that they had two Christmases, and even now when I'm on an assignment, I usually tell the producer or the director that I can't work today because it's January 7 and that's my Christmas.

# Henry Mancini

AMILY GATHERINGS HAVE BEEN THE essence of my Christmases for as far back as I can remember. In the early thirties in West Aliquippa, Pennsylvania, my dad, mother, and I would pack into the family Model T Ford and drive the one hundred miles to Cleveland to visit my uncle Fred and aunt Tre. The gatherings at their home were always warm and festive. With all the Italian cooks in the family, the special Christmas food never stopped coming. This happened every year until I left for the service at the age of eighteen.

Later, after Ginny and I were married, and our three children were able to travel, we spent many of our early Christmases at the Royal Hawaiian Hotel in Honolulu. In the mid-sixties we started going to Sun Valley for our holidays. Our son, Chris, and daughters, Monica and Felice, readily took to skiing as did Ginny and I. In the early seventies we began going to Vail, which we have continued to do every year at Christmastime. Our group has grown steadily with the addition of Felice's husband, Doug Brenberg, Chris's wife, Analei, and our three grandchildren, Christopher, Lelia, and Luca. Ginny and I look forward to these very special times with the family.

# Johnny Mathis

CHRISTMAS HAS ALWAYS BEEN A special family time for me, especially when I was growing up in San Francisco—and music always played a major role. My parents worked for a wealthy San Francisco family as domestics, supporting me and my six brothers and sisters. We weren't poor—we just didn't have any money. I attended George Washington High School and sang in the choir. During the holidays everything was fair game—we sang in the shopping malls, in the department stores; we even sang in as many as four different churches on Sunday as well as a couple of local synagogues.

Later, in my twenties, when I was in New York City recording for Columbia Records, I'll never forget recording what was the first of numerous Christmas albums. It was the middle of a sweltering, muggy July in the city. The temperature and the humidity were both in the high nineties. We were recording in a lovely old church, noted for its wonderful acoustics, but all of us were feeling far from cheery. Suddenly Percy Faith, who was our producer, burst into the church all bundled up in a huge coat and muffler and gloves and began tossing confetti all over me and all the musicians—well, we all just fell apart with laughter. Now, every time I hear a song from the LP, I can't help smiling.

The only thing I'm not fond of at Christmas is hearing myself so much.

# Captain Eugene ("Red") McDaniel,

## USN, Ret.

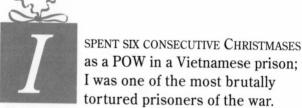

**I** SPENT SIX CONSECUTIVE CHRISTMASES as a POW in a Vietnamese prison; I was one of the most brutally tortured prisoners of the war. Thoughts of family were strong, and the empty, heavy feeling of loneliness would hang hares. Of course, the North Vietnamese had their propaganda room where we had to go on Christmas. There they had gifts for us, and coffee and tea along with a talk with the camp commander. But even this was distorted for their own use. When we would sit down, the camp commander would say, "Even though you have bombed the Vietnamese people, and even though your government murders innocent women and children, we will still allow you to celebrate Christmas."

This, of course, rubbed us the wrong way, and we would never take anything they offered us.

In 1970, when we had fifty-seven men in a compound, we started planning the Christmas week early. We would plan each night of

Christmas week: one night we would have a Christmas miracle story; the next night the Charles Dickens Christmas story; some nights skits were put on by various teams. And we also put together our own choir. I would deliver the Christmas message on Christmas Eve.

For our Christmas treat we would take the rice-straw mats we slept on and hang them on the wall. Then we took our olive-green socks—the VC combat socks given to us—and put them on that mat in the form of a tree. We'd decorate those socks with whitewash. On some Christmases we took pieces of paper, made ornaments out of them, and hung them in the corner of the room in the form of a Christmas tree. It wasn't much, but there was enough symbolism there to give us the spirit. And on Christmas morning, at around five o'clock, "Santa" would appear and we would distribute gifts. Nothing very fancy, of course. A man who didn't smoke would give his cigarettes as the gift for a man who did; the man who smoked would give candy to a third person.

I couldn't express the beauty of those Christmases, the sharing of the little things we had—a cookie, a few pieces of candy the VC had given us—and to see each man's eyes light up, the smile come on his face, to sense the intimate gestures, the deep meaning, the profound simplicity that made it so beautiful. I don't know of any other Christmases that have meant more to me.

# Ali MacGraw

**I** LOVE CHRISTMAS. I LOVE IT THE WAY only a child whose family made a big fuss over it can love it. It is hard for me to remember back to when I first stopped believing in Santa Claus, but I have never stopped believing in Christmas.

In my mind, forever, Christmas is white, and it is charged with a kind of excitement that only a child knows. My parents didn't have much money, and so from the beginning our gifts to each other were mostly handmade. All except for a fabulous electric train that Daddy cursed and labored over until the small hours of Christmas morning. Each year a new car was added, or a special railroad crossing; those were my brother's big present. The important thing was for it to run smoothly, perfectly, around and around, under the big mahogany table that held our tree. And no matter how many times we crept down those stairs as little children for our first peak at Christmas, that train would make us gasp.

My "big" present one year was a dollhouse, every bit of which my parents made, and added to year after year. They papered the walls with special paper, and my mother dressed the dolls in new clothes; together my parents made tiny plates of enameled copper, and knives and forks of pewter. Year-round, the dollhouse had a special place under a sideboard. It was my favorite toy.

I love Christmas, but I am stuck with an over-the-top level of expectation as I get older. I guess that it has taken me a long time to realize how painful the holiday can be for anyone who has had a difficult childhood, and I have often chosen men whose own memories were painful. When Josh was little, he loved it, but as he grows older, he thinks of it more and more as a holiday for little children. I try to remember that Christmas is, above all, a celebration for the birthday of someone who taught us the meaning of real compassion and unconditional love.

I try to have as many people around as possible, and to remember only the good parts of my own childhood. I guess I try to fill the void left in my heart when Josh got to the age when he could no longer be fooled, when, perhaps, he began to mourn for his own loss of innocence.

And I ache for every person who is alone at Christmas—for the stranger, of course, but also for the people whom I have hurt, upon whose lives and hearts I have inadvertently trampled, in my impatience for perfection. I cry every Christmas night, just as I did as a child, feeling the special night slip away for another year, leaving a poor old tree to sit naked and dry in the driveway, and the wonderful old ornaments to sleep in their cotton batting until next year.

Christmas makes me long for that impossible thing: for every person on earth to be fed and clothed and sheltered—and loved.

# Rachel McLish

**M**Y BABY SISTER AND I USED TO THINK that God was constantly playing a cruel trick on us. My whole family for that matter. We didn't have a fireplace, so what was the point of Christmas stockings? Not to mention the anxiety about no place for Santa to park, or if he would even bother to stop by. And no matter how hard we prayed for snow, even if it was just to get a glimpse of it, it would usually be close to 80°. Santa in surfing trunks? Gimme a break. I hated those cards. The Rio Grande Valley of south Texas was certainly not the stuff that Christmas anything was made of.

So off we'd go to our grandparents' house. They knew how to do Christmas right. The spray snow on the windows, colored lights along the porch, Christmas knickknacks everywhere. As we pulled up in our car, we'd usually scramble out over each other the instant the car was turned off and literally race to the door. No competition here. "Hi, Lelo; hi, Lela." Kiss, kiss; hug, hug. "Hi, Rugy; hi, Robert, Richard, Roland"—our cousins were already there.

Lela and her friends had done their thing again. It's kind of like an annual quilting bee, only they make hundreds of tamales. One lady would smear, the next would stuff, then fold, then stack—the tamale assembly line. Tamales for Christmas dinner, tamales for gifts, for snacks, for breakfast—who started that tradition anyway? And dessert?...*capirotada!* Oh, yuck! No way are we eating that! Nobody in their right mind would eat *capirotada.* It looked nasty and it had raisins. I hated raisins.

There was still time to goof around and play games before everyone went to midnight Mass. The fact that I got to stay up so late on Christmas Eve was thrilling to me. The butterflies would go from my stomach to my heart and back again. Even as a child, I sensed that Christmastime was a blessed time, sacred. It was magical to me and it built hope. It was good to believe in God and to thank him for Baby Jesus. It gave Christmas a reason for being. Somehow, the snow didn't matter, the chimney didn't matter. It never did.

# Ed McMahon

THE MOST UNUSUAL CHRISTMAS I REMEM-
ber was one that happened quite by
accident. I had been selected as a
naval aviation cadet and was told by
the navy to remain at home until it was my turn to be
called into active duty to start my aviation career in
the military. While awaiting my orders, I took a job
at the War Department working on a surveyors'
crew. We were busy expanding a military air base
near my home in Lowell, Massachusetts.

Because I was "going off to war," my mother
decided that we would have no formal Christmas in
our home. It would "just be too sad." So there was to
be no tree and no decorations. My father and I went
along with her wishes reluctantly.

On Christmas Eve day I was busy on the
surveyors' crew extending the runway at the air
base. We happened to be going through a nursery,
and directly in front of us was the most beautiful six-
foot-tall Christmas tree I had ever seen—a blue
spruce. I said to one of my assistants, "Let me have
that ax, I'll get this one." I adroitly chopped down
that Christmas tree and arrived at our front door
with it over my shoulder.

I set about trying to convince my mother that
this was some kind of an omen and we should have a
tree this year. And when she finally agreed, we
wound up having the most wonderful Christmas
before I went off to war.

# Ari Meyers

*I*N THE FILM *IT'S A WONDERFUL LIFE,* George's realization at the end of this movie of what a meaningful life he had really led is not only a lesson in the rewards of sacrifice and selflessness, but an example of how accepting the situation we are faced with and living fully within those circumstances is the key to being happy.

# Sir John Mills

**T**HE CHRISTMAS I REMEMBER MOST vividly was that of 1939. I was, at the time, a sapper or private soldier in the Royal Engineers. We were stationed at a camp in Hertfordshire about fifty miles from London. The living quarters were primitive to say the least of it. I occupied a hut eighteen feet by twelve feet with eleven other loyal soldiers of the King.

The weather that year was appalling by any standards, arcticlike conditions with the thermometer well below zero.

We were an antiaircraft battery and "stood to" every evening from dusk to dawn. On that particular Christmas Eve, I decided to cause a diversion by blowing a temperature of 104°. The MO took me off duty and ordered me to bed, the bed being a straw palliasse with lumps like concrete in it.

I awoke at about two A.M. feeling really

lousy with a bladder at bursting point. While I was struggling with my battle dress in preparation for the journey to the latrine, which was situated in the corner of the field some fifty yards away, the door opened and my friend Scotty appeared. He took one look at me and said, "What the hell do you think you're doing? It's cold enough to freeze the nuts off a brass monkey out there. Get right back into bed."

"But Scotty," I said, "I've got to take a leak."

He reached for a gun boot and handed it to me: "No problem, Johnny Boy, be my guest."

I accepted the offer gratefully. The relief was enormous. "I can't thank you enough, Scotty," I said. "You've saved my life."

My friend from over the border smiled. "Don't thank me. Thank the sergeant. That's his bloody boot."

# Juliet Mills

*A CHRISTMAS MEMORY*

CHRISTMAS HAS ALWAYS BEEN A VERY special time for our family, a time when we all try to be in the same place at the same time. Whether that means driving many miles, or flying across oceans, I have many wonderful childhood memories of Christmases spent all over the world.

One of my memories of an English Christmas is the carol singers who come and sing outside your front door on Christmas Eve. They'd ring the bell, and when you opened the door, there they would be, like a Christmas card, dressed in bright colors, muffled up from the cold, carrying their lanterns and singing all those beautiful Christmas carols. Afterward, my parents would serve some of their famous Christmas punch and send them reeling on their way! Then we would go back into the warm house and roast chestnuts on the fire. And we would wait for the sound of the bells tinkling on Santa's sleigh, and rush into bed when we heard them.

122

# Dudley Moore

*I* WAS ALWAYS TRANSFIXED BY THE BEAUTY of the season when I was in England, and I remember being enchanted on at least one occasion at the falling of snow on Christmas morning for the first time that year. It was a wonderful experience.

My Christmas usually consisted of going to my local church, where I was organist and occasionally in the choir, indulging in my favorite pastime...which was the singing and playing of hymns. I enjoyed so much the beautiful decorations in the church and all of the festivities, which promised wonderfully colorful social events. I always enjoyed the food, which was rich, fatty, and sleep-giving!

I remember one Christmas getting my first watch and being endlessly intrigued by the sound of its ticking. I still retain that same magical feeling about watches. Also, about Cox's Orange Pippin apples, which used to come about that time of year! I'm afraid all of those times were wonderful to me. Times of great happiness, brought together by wonderful radio broadcasts, which always seemed to pop up that time of year. Music, color, and endless gregariousness, which seemed to pervade the scene beautifully. I miss those scenes and yet they are available, but they will never have quite the same magic I'm sure.

# Roger Moore

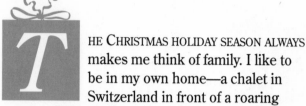

*T*HE CHRISTMAS HOLIDAY SEASON ALWAYS makes me think of family. I like to be in my own home—a chalet in Switzerland in front of a roaring fireplace. I have never not been there except for once in twenty-eight years. Last year my family spent the holiday with Michael Caine and his family outside Oxford, England.

Christmas dinner was prepared by Michael, who is a wonderful cook…almost as good as I am. December 25 is the one day out of the year that my wife, Luisa, allows me near the kitchen to cook. In spite of my belief in my culinary abilities, on that day especially, our dinner may not be perfect, but it's prepared with love.

# Richard Nixon

 I SHALL NEVER FORGET CHRISTMASTIME 1956, when I visited some of the refugees who flooded into Austria in the wake of the Soviet's brutal suppression of the Hungarian uprising. Thousands hoped to come to the United States. Because of the season it was particularly ironic that many Americans, concerned that these newcomers would snap up scarce jobs, felt there was no more room in the land of the free for those fleeing tyranny.

For individuals, a lesson of the Christmas story is that we must open our homes and hearts to those in need. For a great, prosperous, and free nation such as ours, it is that the duty of a free people is to work to extend freedom to others.

*Richard Nixon*
4-20-89

# Charles Osgood

A T CHRISTMASTIME ONE YEAR WHEN I was just a little guy, I thought I saw a tear in some grown-up person's eye. And I couldn't understand why such a thing as that should be at a time that seemed so happy and so wonderful to me.

And I asked this grown-up person if anything was wrong, and I was told...it's only that the lights were bright and strong. And indeed it did seem dazzling, the way the lights were strung, and it seemed bright and magical to anyone so young.

My grandparents were there, of course, my dad and mother, too, and lots of aunts and uncles—there were more than just a few—and my brother and my sister and some friends who would stop by, and we'd sing the Christmas carols about angels heard on high.

"O Little Town of Bethlehem," and always "Silent Night," I suppose it was old-fashioned and that some might think it trite, but World War II was going on...with battles raging then, and yet we sang of peace on earth and of goodwill to men.

The yuletide log was burning with a warm and lovely glow. I can almost feel it now although it was so long ago. It's Christmastime again now, we have children of our own, and the little boy I used to be is long since fully grown.

And I found myself the other night just

looking at the tree and thinking about Christmas past and how it used to be. An old familiar carol on the stereo was playing, and suddenly I realized what a little voice was saying.

"It's Merry Christmas time," he said, "the season to be glad. But I saw you for a moment and I thought you looked so sad. Is anything the matter? Is everything all right?"

"Oh, sure"—I smiled—"I guess my eyes were dazzled by the light."

# Dolly Parton

**M**Y FONDEST CHRISTMAS MEMORIES HAVE always been about being together with family and fixing good things to eat. Whether it's Christmas or any holiday, here's my personal recipe for my favorite dessert, Islands in the Stream.

## 🍃 *Dolly Parton's Islands in the Stream* 🍃

1 quart milk
3 large eggs, separated
2/3 cup sugar
2 heaping teaspoons flour
1 teaspoon vanilla extract

🍃

In a 2-quart saucepan, heat milk just until bubbles form around side of pan. In small bowl with electric beater, cream egg yolks and 1/3 cup sugar until smooth and pale yellow. Beat in flour. Beat hot milk into yolk mixture until blended. Pour milk mixture back into saucepan and cook, stirring constantly, until it thickens, 20–25 minutes. Take custard off heat and stir in vanilla. Cover surface with plastic wrap; refrigerate until cold.

In large skillet, heat an inch of water to boiling and continue to simmer. In bowl with electric mixer, beat egg whites until soft peaks form. Gradually beat in remaining 1/3 cup sugar until stiff peaks form.

With large spoon, scoop up one-sixth of beaten egg whites into a large oval. With the help of another spoon, push oval into simmering water. Poach egg-white ovals, 3 at a time, until set, about 5 minutes, gently turning them twice. Remove carefully and drain on paper towels. Repeat to make 3 more.

To serve, pour chilled custard into shallow serving bowl. Float islands of egg-white ovals on top. Sprinkle ground nutmeg on top of the islands, if desired. Chill dessert until serving time. Serves 6.

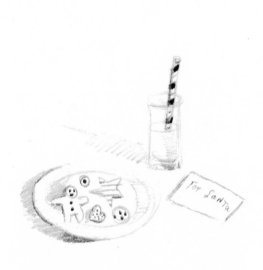

# Dr. Norman Vincent Peale

THE MAGIC MESSAGE OF CHRISTMAS IS that God gives us so much more than we can possibly give back! He gave the world the greatest gift of all time. "For unto us a child is born, unto us a Son is given." (Isaiah 9:6)

# Suzanne Pleshette

THIS POEM WAS WRITTEN TO MY husband, Tom Gallagher. It was his only present from me this particular Christmas. We'd lost half of our house in a mud slide, and all of our money was tied up in trying to rebuild. There was nothing left for gifts so we decided to forgo Christmas. But on Christmas Eve, Tommy produced the saddest little Christmas tree you've ever seen, which we decorated with tender loving care, and I gave him this poem. We've never had a better Christmas!

*Would that we had riches*
*Beyond the wildest reason,*
*I'd fashion you a Christmas*
*So joyful for this season.*
*But since the coffer's empty*
*And the gifts are not to be,*
*I give you all my love, dear*
*And I give you freely, me.*

# Sidney Poitier

*I*N A MATTER OF MONTHS THE FACE OF MY oldest brother, an illegal alien who as a teenager had entered the U.S. without proper papers and was living and working in Miami, Florida, had started to grow fuzzy in my recollection. The family he left behind was as poor as one could imagine. I was seven that year and was working from sunup to sundown in the tomato fields on Cat Island in the Bahamas to pull my share of the survival load. As the months of his absence approached a full year, I, the youngest of eight, could barely remember what he looked like.

Then came Christmas and his spirit in my mind's eye became as crystal clear as any image any child has ever had of Santa Claus. My brother's name is Cyril. He worked as a domestic for wealthy families on Miami Beach. There he would collect the old clothing and footgear discarded by employers who had no further use for them. A cardboard box filled with such odd-lot items arrived at Cat Island in time to mark his first Christmas absent from the family. In it was something for everybody. For me a pair of shoes that were a bit too tight, but I loved them just the same.

Every year that followed throughout my childhood, my brother Santa Claus came through with a cardboard box filled with useful goodies for those he had left behind. And that is my fondest remembrance of Christmas.

# Anthony Quinn

I T WAS THE TWENTY-FOURTH OF December, 1929, and it was raining. The sun was going down on that forgotten land called the east side of Los Angeles. My sister and I were standing out on the porch singing like only kids who are hungry can sing, defiantly...

> *"I'm singing in the rain...*
> *Just singing in the rain...*
> *What a wonderful feeling*
> *I'm happy again."*

The steady rain was turning the clay street to muddy clay—over to the left there was a gully. My mother was painfully trudging up the slippery incline, loaded down with some bags.

At that time she was working for an Italian family doing their housekeeping, cooking, and ironing. But they were very nice to her, and on special days such as  Thanksgiving, Easter, and Christmas they would give her leftover turkey or cake to bring home.

We naturally hoped that there were some gifts for us for Christmas.

We rushed through the rain to meet her

and help her with the bags. My mother said we must wait until the following day to open the bags.

Since my father's death four years before, my sister and I were not used to Christmas presents, and I doubt if she slept one wink more than I that night wondering what mother had brought in those magical bags.

We were up at dawn, but mother said to wait until after breakfast (which was nothing more than coffee and rolled tortillas filled with cheese).

We made a rush for the bags and opened them in what can only kiddingly be called a living room.

My mother handed me one bag and said it was for me, and the other bag was for Stella, my sister. My mother and grandmother divided another bag.

I could hardly believe my eyes. My bag was filled with fine silk shirts with hardly a tear and only a few buttons missing, silk socks, seven or eight ties (slightly wrinkled), but to me they were the finest clothes that I had ever seen.

I put one of the new shirts on. It was a little large, but my grandmother promised she would cut it down to size.

The feeling of silk on my body was like feeling gold dust.

I remember that Italian family as the richest, kindest, and most generous friends. They had given Christmas a meaning.

# Deborah Raffin

**M**Y MOST UNFORGETTABLE CHRISTMAS holiday was in 1981. George Cukor, a friend and legendary motion picture director whom I had had tremendous admiration for almost since birth, spent the holiday with my husband and me at our snowbound Vermont farmhouse. George was eighty-two years old but sixteen years old at heart. Whether it was snowmobile-racing with our Yorkshire terrier, Oscar, on his lap or taking midnight horsesled rides through the pristine

*Photo by Richard Stanley*

countryside, he was always game. A true test of our friendship and George's enjoyment of risk-taking was that he kindly ate the meals that I cooked and actually pretended to like them. For the quintessential curmudgeon, this was quite a show of holiday kindness. What a friend!

On Christmas morning, we exchanged our gifts and delved into our goody-filled stockings. George and his friend Richard Stanley received bright-red Bloomingdale long johns. Later on, after George's midday snooze, he summoned us to his room. There he stood looking like a deranged but adorable elf in his vivid "Bloomie" long johns. It was an especially happy Christmas.

On our way home via Boston, we stopped to have lunch at the Durgin Park Restaurant. As we were leaving, my husband ran ahead to bring our car around. Before he got twenty yards away, we saw two muggers attack him. I stood momentarily stunned. George didn't. Suddenly, one of the muggers found that he had just acquired a headlock from a man several times his age. Perhaps as a result of the shock as much as from anything else, the attackers decided to flee. The police caught and arrested them. George felt that it had indeed been a very good day!

Now, my only twinge of sadness at Christmastime is that George is not with us. I will love and miss him always.

# Rex Reed

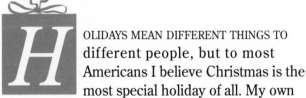

**H**OLIDAYS MEAN DIFFERENT THINGS TO different people, but to most Americans I believe Christmas is the most special holiday of all. My own childhood memories have always been associated with food, friends, and the joy of sharing both. I have never spent a Christmas alone. I like to cook for friends, often taking in all orphans and strays with no place to go, but I'm rather stubborn about what I serve. Cranberries must be fresh for the sauce. My grandmother's Texas corn-bread stuffing has been duplicated faithfully for years.

My favorite Christmas, as what my aunt Charley Lavendar Lorean Calhoun calls a "grown-up, sophisticated, adult-type person," was the year I bought my country house, a 38-acre, 1780 Connecticut farm right out of a Grandma Moses greeting card on an isolated rural road with split-rail fences, a sugar-maple mill, and a trout pond. I moved in on Christmas Eve with one bottle of champagne, one chair, and a sleeping bag. A gang of friends from the city were due on the train at sunset to help me celebrate, bringing with them the ingredients for a lavish Christmas Day feast. The tree was trimmed, the popcorn was ready. Then it started to snow. Lacy flakes, at first. By dusk, a whirling blizzard. Doom and gloom descended with the darkness and I faced a lonely Christmas in front of a wood-burning fireplace with a can of tuna. By ten P.M. ten inches had drowned the landscape with white cake frosting. The roads were closed. The snowplows were stuck. My friends were stranded at the railroad depot.

Then, just before midnight chimes signaled the prelude to Christmas Day, I heard the sound of sleigh bells on the deserted road. My friends had been rescued by a neighboring dairy farmer who jogged them through the storm on a horse-drawn hay wagon. Above the tinkle of the bells, I could hear the merry laughter of happy pilgrims, lugging their sleeping bags and a half-frozen turkey across the drifts of snow, rushing and falling in their united haste, lured like fireflies through the dark toward the lights of Christmas.

# Lee Remick

### CHRISTMAS TREES
**A Christmas
Circular Letter**

The city had withdrawn into itself
And left at last the country to the
country;
When between whirls of snow not
come to lie
And whirls of foliage not yet laid, there drove
A stranger to our yard, who looked the city,
Yet did in country fashion in that there
He sat and waited till he drew us out
A-buttoning coats to ask him who he was.
He proved to be the city come again
To look for something it had left behind
And could not do without and keep its Christmas.
He asked if I would sell my Christmas trees;
My woods—the young fir balsams like a place
Where houses all are churches and have spires.
I hadn't thought of them as Christmas trees.
I doubt if I was tempted for a moment
To sell them off their feet to go in cars
And leave the slope behind the house all bare,
Where the sun shines now no warmer than the moon.
I'd hate to have them know it if I was.
Yet more I'd hate to hold my trees except
As others hold theirs or refuse for them,
Beyond the time of profitable growth,

*The trial by market everything must come to.*
*I dallied so much with the thought of selling.*
*Then whether from mistaken courtesy*
*And fear of seeming short of speech, or whether*
*From hope of hearing good of what was mine,*
*I said, "There aren't enough to be worth while."*

*"I could soon tell how many they would cut,*
*You let me look them over."*

*"You could look.*
*But don't expect I'm going to let you have them."*
*Pasture they spring in, some in clumps too close*
*That lop each other of boughs, but not a few*
*Quite solitary and having equal boughs*
*All round and round. The latter he nodded yes to,*
*Or paused to say beneath some lovelier one,*
*With a buyer's moderation, "That would do."*
*I thought so, too, but wasn't there to say so.*
*We climbed the pasture on the south, crossed over,*
*And came down on the north.*

*He said, "A thousand."*

*"A thousand Christmas trees!—at what apiece?"*
*He felt some need of softening that to me:*
*"A thousand trees would come to thirty dollars."*

*Then I was certain I had never meant*
*To let him have them. Never show surprise!*
*But thirty dollars seemed so small beside*
*The extent of pasture I should strip, three cents*
*(For that was all they figured out apiece),*
*Three cents so small beside the dollar friends*

*I should be writing to within the hour*
*Would pay in cities for good trees like those,*
*Regular vestry trees whole Sunday schools*
*Could hang enough on to pick off enough.*
*A thousand Christmas trees I didn't know I had!*
*Worth three cents more to give away than sell*
*As may be shown by a simple calculation.*
*Too bad I couldn't lay one in a letter.*
*I can't help wishing I could send you one*
*In wishing you herewith a merry Christmas.*

# Line Renaud

*I*T WAS VERY DIFFICULT FOR ME TO HAVE A merry Christmas when I was a little girl. My family was very poor. We lived in Armentières in the north of France at the Belgium border on the main highway that goes from Lille to Dunkerque. My father was a truck driver for a clothing factory, my mother a stenographer in another textile factory. I was brought up by my great-grandmother who lived with us in what we called the *corons,* that is to say, houses lined up in a row, all the same, very plain, without bathrooms, with only a sink that had no running water.

To get the water, we had to go to the pump, which was behind the row of houses in the center of the street. My mother, in order to help augment the monthly income, worked after hours as a hairdresser from house to house. This region in the north of France was the coldest, foggiest, windiest, most tempestuous. The landscape was the mountains formed by the leftover residue from the coal mines. So, Christmases were very cold.

My saddest Christmas was after the declaration of war in 1939 when my father, like all of the fathers, had to leave to defend France from the German enemy. We did not know then that we were not going to see him for four and a half years. Like many French people, he was taken prisoner in the German camps. There was a long time without news from him; we thought he was dead or that he had disappeared forever. The sadness invaded our household, and soon our village and all of France were occupied by the German army as well. During those four years, whenever I could, I would go around the neighborhood singing in order to try to bring a little joy.

The years passed, I grew from a little girl to a pretty young lady, and finally, at the time of the liberation, at fifteen years old, I was singing everywhere for charities to benefit the POWs' children. In this little corner of France, I became well-known. Some fathers came back from Germany, but we still had no news from my father. Would he return?

Christmas Eve 1945, I was singing in Lille, still as an amateur of course, always to benefit the families and the children of the POWs. That afternoon, I was onstage, all made up, with a hairdo like Veronica Lake's (the GIs had made her famous by the films that, at last, were coming from America, rather than the ones from Germany we saw during the occupation). In spite of my young age, I was singing torch songs, written by a very famous composer in France who can be compared in the United States to perhaps a Cole Porter or an Irving Berlin. His name was Louis Gasté. I loved his songs, so therefore, I sang them everywhere. So during this Christmas Eve day, I was in the midst of singing with all my heart and soul, when suddenly in the back of the hall, someone began to cry out my name while coming down the center aisle of the room.

"Jacqueline, Jacqueline, stop. Your father is here. He is back from Germany, and he is here looking all over for you." And there was my father, who had left me at the age of ten, a little girl, returning to find me as a young lady of fifteen. He climbed on stage, he hugged me in his arms, and he could not believe his eyes. I, Jacqueline, as an almost-grown-up young lady, with makeup, singing and by now crying, as was everyone else in the audience.

This memory with my daddy will always be the most beautiful Christmas memory of my life.

P.S. I forgot to tell you that since then I have had many merry Christmases with Louis Gasté, the composer whom, as a child, I loved, who became my husband and still is after forty years now. The most beautiful song that he wrote to our love is called "Feelings."

# Burt Reynolds

**C**HRISTMAS HAS NEVER BEEN THE SAME since we began sharing that special day with our son, Quinton. Actually it's just one of many wonderful cherished days that we now share because of him. We wish you a merry Christmas.

*Love, Quinton and What's-his-name*

# Fred Rogers

OUR TWO SONS ALWAYS LOOKED FORWARD to going out to get the Christmas tree and decorating it. From the time they were big enough to stand up, they helped with hanging the ornaments. Those early years when we finished, the bottom branches were always laden with decorations, and the top, which the adults decorated, was relatively bare. Our favorite ornaments are still those the boys made in nursery school. I'm particularly fond of one Jay made out of wood and tied together with rope. Chef Brockett, who appears regularly on *Mister Rogers' Neighborhood,* and his wife always stop by our house at Christmastime. They are very artistic people whose tree is invariably a work of art. Don and Leslie often make fun of our tree. "Well," they'll say, "this year we'll give it a C-plus." Ours is usually a homely tree, but it suits us fine.

From earliest childhood, our young son John insisted on helping drag the tree out of the car and putting it on its stand. And every year as we came in the door, he heard his grandmother Byrd call out, "Did you get any loose branches for me?" (She used those extra branches to decorate the mantelpiece.) The first Christmas John was big enough to bring the tree in all by himself, he came in hollering, "Hey, Nana Byrd, I got you some loose branches!"

At moments like these you realize how much family traditions mean to children and how very important the little things are to you.

# Kenny
# and
# Marianne Rogers

**O**NE OF OUR MOST MEMORABLE CHRIST-mases was the year Christopher was two. He was excited about Christmas so we took him to see Santa. Although he sat on his lap and had his picture taken, he was actually scared of him and cried. After that, he wouldn't go to Kenny for about two weeks because he looked too much like Santa. But when Christmas came and Santa left Christopher with some wonderful toys, he decided he liked Santa after all (not to mention Kenny).

# Wayne Rogers

M Y FONDEST MEMORIES OF CHRISTMAS center around my children. As soon as they were able to know the meaning of words, each Christmas Eve I would read them "The Night Before Christmas." We have continued this little ritual, and now that they are adults, every Christmas Eve it is mandatory that we sit by the fire and I read to them as if they were still little ones. In fact, when I look at their faces, they seem to revert back to those first years of childish fascination, smiling and laughing at the Santa Claus they hold so dearly in their memory.

# Mickey Rooney

*I*T SEEMS TO ME THAT RUNNING AROUND shopping malls, buying Christmas presents, doesn't make you a Christian any more than going to a garage makes a car.

# Gena Rowlands

**W**HEN YOU'RE A CHILD, CHRISTMAS comes before itself. It comes when you see a half-remembered look in the eyes of a friend, family member, or even a stranger; mouths try not to smile, yet can't help themselves. When they see you, they make the lower lip overlap the upper as if to hold in a secret.

Again you hear sounds of bells you've heard before, not bells tolling in belfries, but small tinkly bells from people passing you in the street. Auto horns make sassy toot-toots instead of warning blasts.

Christmas is the time of hidden hopes tiptoeing out from their hiding, a door suddenly closes, footsteps run lightly, but fast, a dresser drawer makes a muffled squeak, is hurriedly opened and quickly closes.

Christmas is the fragrance of cinnamon. It is the mystery of unseen truths, in ordinary things going on daily that are tied to a far earlier time: a time of promise.

# Pat Sajak

**F**OR SHEER EXCITEMENT, IT WOULD BE difficult to top the Christmas of 1989. There I was in Maryland with my wife-to-be and her family, and our wedding was just one week away. Outside the kitchen window we could see the not-yet-completed tent in the snow-covered backyard. Seven nights later, 150 guests would be filling up that tent to ring in the New Year and the beginning of a new life for Lesly and me. As we gathered around the family Christmas tree, I have to admit that my mind was less on the gifts we were opening than on whether my tuxedo would fit properly, bad weather would prevent out-of-towners from traveling to the wedding, the cake would be ready on time, and a thousand other details. In the end, everything went beautifully. I'll always look back at the Christmas of 1989 as the beginning of the most exciting and wonderful time of my life.

# Steve Sax

CHRISTMAS HAS ALWAYS BEEN ONE OF MY favorite times of the year. I remember as a child receiving a baseball glove and bat on Christmas and rushing outside to play catch with my brother and to fantasize about making it to the big leagues someday. (I grew up in Sacramento, so even though it was cold outside on Christmas Day, the weather was acceptable for playing ball year-round.)

I am now blessed with a wonderful wife, Debbie, and two healthy children, Lauren and John. My fantasies of playing major league baseball have also come true. It's sort of overwhelming to think about it all, and I now look upon Christmas as a time to give thanks for all of the good things that have happened to me. For several years now, my wife and I have visited local hospitals on Christmas, to visit with children and other patients who cannot spend the holiday with their families. I pass out autographed posters and photos and derive pleasure and satisfaction from the joy and happiness I see from the young faces.

Making these visits has become a tradition in the Sax household, and I feel as if I benefit as much as anyone in participating. It really is an opportunity for me to give thanks for the blessings in my life and to help those who are in need of some extra love on this special day. I look forward to meeting many more people in the coming years.

# Arnold Scaasi

**M**Y FONDEST MEMORY OF CHRISTMAS IS as a little boy living in Montreal, Canada, where I was brought up in a Jewish family that never formally celebrated the holiday. Of course, Christmas was all around us: in school, in the shops, and especially in the snow-covered streets, which looked like Christmas cards with all the decorations. We had a balcony outside my mother's bedroom, and something I remember that made Christmas special for me was when the carolers came to sing amidst the falling snow "It Came Upon a Midnight Clear." We would bundle up and stand on the balcony and listen to the beautiful music. My mother would go downstairs and open the front door and give cakes and candies to the carolers. It was all so jolly and friendly and has always seemed to me what Christmas is truly about.

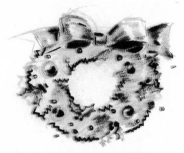

# Francesco Scavullo

*I* HAVE NEVER LOST MY ENTHUSIASM FOR the annual miracle of Christmas. As the years pass, I continue to anticipate this marvelous time of grace with the same enthusiasm I experienced as a child. Autumn is a busy and often stressful period, so the peace and serenity of the Christmas holiday with its implicit promise of seeing beloved family and friends provide welcome relief and spiritual refreshment. There is the cherished sense of renewal and forgiveness in the message of nativity: the feeling that we are all very much loved.

# Captain Walter M. ("Wally") Schirra, Jr.

*I*T WAS DECEMBER 1965. TOM STAFFORD and I were piloting *Gemini VI* on a mission to rendezvous with *Gemini VII* and maintain station. On December 16, after successfully completing our mission, we headed back to Earth.

Three hours before retrofire, with all serious intent, Tom and I decided to do our high jinks for the day. At 0600 Houston time we were crossing the California coast. We began the day by broadcasting to Mission Control in Houston that we had sighted an unidentified flying object (UFO) that seemed to be on a collision course. Chaos ran amok at

Mission Control. They got on the phone trying to see who it could be...Russia?

Stafford suddenly said he saw "what appears to be eight small modules pulling a large spacecraft...there is an astronaut in a red space suit." He began to play tiny bells, bringing them closer to the microphone as he played. I picked up my Hohner harmonica and played "Jingle Bells."

The prank was one of the highest-class "gotcha's" of all time, but most appropriate for that Christmas 1965. It's a tale to share with children, to let them know that even astronauts encounter Santa Claus. •

# Paul Scofield

**M**Y OWN RECOLLECTIONS OF CHILDHOOD Christmases are blurred and hazy. I never recall a white one; they come back to me as warm and replete, lit by wavering gaslight—a sheltered time without the harshnesses that children dread. Later, when my own children were small, my chief memories are of seas of wrapping paper and Strauss waltzes on the record player in the morning—and champagne!

# Eric Sevareid

I USED TO PRINT THESE FEW LINES ON MY Christmas cards in the years when I sent them out. I don't know who wrote the lines. One story was that they were written several centuries ago by a monk. Later, that they were actually written in America, author unknown, in this century.

"There is nothing I can give which you have not; but there is much that, while I cannot give, you can take. No heaven can come to us unless our hearts find rest in it today. Take heaven. No peace lies in the future which is not hidden in this present instant. Take peace. The gloom of the world is but a shadow; behind it, yet within reach, is joy. Take joy. And so, at this Christmastime, I greet you with the prayer that for you, now and forever, the day breaks and the shadows flee away."

# Martin Sheen

*T*HE ANTICIPATION OF CHRISTMAS 1951 was muddled and bleak indeed, what with the death of my mother five months earlier, one brother off to California, another in Korea with the Marines, and the remaining eight of us (seven boys and one girl) living in a small, two-story house on Brown Street with my father, a hardworking Spanish immigrant who carried his heavy grief deep within himself.

There was far more preparation for the great feast done outside the home, at school, at church, at the Boys Club, as well as the homes of friends, and it was the first Christmas in memory that approached with no great sense of excitement. In fact, I can't recall having bought anyone in the family a gift, save the usual "two-set hanky" for Pop and a few trinkets for the long row of stockings hung on the fireplace mantel.

Right up to Christmas Eve, there was no tree present in our home, and no plans known to any of us that one would imminently appear. My father spent most of the day shopping for the Christmas meal, and when he returned midafternoon without a tree, not one of us dared make mention of the assumed oversight.

By nightfall, we had accepted the reality that there simply wasn't going to be a Christmas tree in our house this year.

Who could have predicted an appearance by the notorious alcoholic housepainter Henry Walker, known to everyone in the neighborhood for his rollicking high jinks and outrageous public disputes with the long-suffering Mrs. Walker and their two grown sons who still lived at home.

The inebriated Mr. Walker arrived at our front door around nine P.M. pounding and shouting for my father. "Frank," he yelled. "Come out here and see what all I brought ya!"

Certain we were being drawn into another domestic quarrel with the Walker family, my father approached the door with great trepidation and with all of us at his heels. When he swung open the door, lo and behold—there stood a broad-smiling Henry holding a huge tree to my father's arms. My father was dumbfounded, but before he could collect his wits, Henry was stumbling down the front porch steps with a laugh and disappeared into the chilly night air.

We never knew where he got that beautiful Christmas tree or how he knew we were treeless that year. We simply accepted it much as the poor often accept such things at such times from such people.

And I cannot recall a Christmas thereafter until I left home eight years later that a large, full tree was not personally delivered to our house by that infamous and equally beloved friend and neighbor, Henry Walker.

# Sidney Sheldon

Christmas is the time
 For love of family,
 The love of friends,
 The love of our fellow men,
 And the love of parents,
But most of all,
 Christmas is for the children.

# Dinah Shore

*I*'LL USE ALMOST ANY EXCUSE FOR A special-occasion dinner, but Christmas and Thanksgiving are naturals. I must confess to you that they are just about the same, but since they only occur twice a year and my family seems to insist upon it with a little help from me, the menu remains virtually the same for both Christmas and Thanksgiving. For instance, you must have corn-bread stuffing for the turkey with enough left over to make crisp patties surrounding the fowl. I invariably make some absolutely beautiful cranberry mold and serve plain old jellied cranberry slices on a larger slice of unpeeled orange. The vegetable may vary—broccoli and cauliflower mixed with a few red peppers for color. Good old green beans Southern style and then, of course, mashed potatoes and/or sweet potato puffs. I always have a pecan pie, and I'll alternate sweet potato pie or pumpkin pie depending on whether or not I have served the sweet potato puffs or just plain mashed potatoes. Whipped cream is served on the side, naturally.

## ❧ *Menu* ❧

Chopped Liver served with Rye Toasts

Roast Turkey with Corn-bread Stuffing

Mashed Potatoes and Gravy

Sweet Potato Puffs

Broccoli and Cauliflower with Red Pepper Strips
or Southern-Style Green Beans

Jellied Cranberry Slices on Unpeeled
Orange Slices

Cranberry and Apple Mold

Pecan Pie

Pumpkin or Sweet Potato Pie

Whipped Cream

❧

# Pam Shriver

**T**O ME, CHRISTMAS IS A HOLIDAY MOST enjoyed by kids. When I think of Christmas, I remember the holidays when I was about six years old. I could never sleep on Christmas Eve. I'd lie awake in bed, waiting and listening for Santa Claus's sled to land on the roof. The excitement and anticipation of opening presents and celebrating with my family kept me psyched up—almost like now when I'm going to play a big tennis match.

My older sister, Marion, and I would tiptoe into our grandmother's room early in the morning and talk to her. We'd ask if she thought Santa had really found our chimney and left us a lot of presents. We would wonder aloud about whether or not we had been good enough to deserve any gifts.

Once dressed, we'd venture downstairs to

find a full stocking for every member of the family. One year we only found switches instead of the stockings, and Marion and I were scared that we had been naughty and not nice. But our parents found where Santa had hidden them.

Always after opening our stocking gifts we would have a big breakfast of pears, coffee cake, dove (my father hunts and dove has always been a Christmas breakfast tradition in the Shriver family), and eggs. After breakfast and cleanup, we would head into the living room, where the tree was all lit up and surrounded with presents. We used to feel guilty about Santa's generosity!

In the afternoon, we'd spend time visiting relatives and we'd always have a traditional turkey dinner that night. It was always so sad that we had to wait another 365 days for the next Christmas.

# Ruben Sierra

**A**LTHOUGH ONLY SEVEN YEARS OF AGE, my recollection of December 31, 1972, is horrifyingly vivid and still very haunting.

My boyhood idol, and Puerto Rico's hero, Roberto Clemente, was flying to Nicaragua to aid the survivors of a devastating earthquake. The nation was decimated and Clemente was airlifting vital medical and food supplies, as well as $250,000 he had raised for this relief effort.

Roberto's cargo plane crashed shortly after takeoff, and an eerie pall was cast over the island of Puerto Rico. "El Carnival" ended instantly, and I remember crying for days.

Clemente was larger than life and gave inspiration to all men, regardless of their interest in baseball. He transcended the sport and died expressing his love and concern for his fellow man.

Every Christmas, I reflect on Roberto's altruism and try to mirror his philanthropy.

# Gene Siskel/
# Roger Ebert

## GENE SISKEL:

**H**OLIDAYS ARE GREAT EXCUSES FOR VOIDING grudges and for telling those you live and work with precisely how much they mean to you.

And for at least that moment you can be at peace with the world and yourself.

## ROGER EBERT:

**T**HE MOST UNDERRATED CHRISTMAS film is *A Christmas Story* with its memories of growing up in northern Indiana. I especially love the scene where Santa kicks the kid down the slide as he's asking for the Daisy Red Rider BB-Gun.

# Jaclyn Smith

## THE MAGIC OF CHRISTMAS

Dear Gaston and
Spencer Margaret,

Yes, Santa Claus *does* come down the chimney, and there *are* eight tiny reindeer. They live in your hearts… and in mine, when I see them in your eyes.

And yes, there are Christmas trees from enchanted forests.

There are handmade ornaments, sprinkled with fairy dust blown by a kiss.

Photo by Alana Voeller

*169*

There are nutcrackers that march, and candy canes and sugar plums that dance.

There are lights so bright, the sky adds new stars each night.

There are beautiful moments, wrapped in bright, warm memories.

There *is* magic to Christmas, because you two make the magic happen.

With you, every day is Christmas.

I love you,

Mama

# Liz Smith

CHRISTMAS INDUCES SUCH A FRANTIC feeling in all of us as we rush toward the holidays, making plans, buying gifts, worrying about wrapping and mailing. It has always seemed to me if you aren't ready by Christmas Eve, forget it. But that may be because Christmas Eve was when we (my family in Texas) really celebrated

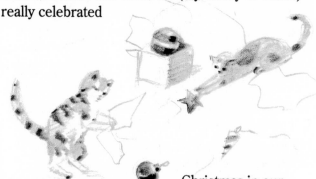

Christmas in our house. Christmas Day was an aftermath, an afterthought, a time to straighten up and begin thinking about the next workday.

So we always had an early supper, slightly festive on Christmas Eve, and then we sat down in the living room to open our gifts. The tree was lit and meaningful because it was night. It was the night of the Savior's birth. My mother would read us the Christmas story from the St. James Bible's chapter of Luke. We would say a prayer and hold hands and say "Amen!" Then we opened our gifts from each other. My father always gave us a silver dollar, which we enjoyed very much, and that was when a silver dollar meant something.

Sometimes one of us or the grandchildren would perform something—"The Night Before Christmas" or "Rudolph the Red-Nosed Reindeer" or "I Saw Mommy Kissing Santa Claus." This added some zip to the proceedings because it was so utterly silly and amateurish. But we were together. We were a family. And then on Christmas morning, Santa would have come for whatever children we were lucky enough to have with us. And we would go to church and spend the rest of the day being lazy and looking at our new things.

I will never forget my mother reading from Luke. My father handing out silver dollars, my brothers both making a little fun of everything, but pleased inside that it was happening. Now I try to celebrate Christmas as much as I can in the same way. It isn't the same anymore. But I still hold the memory of that special night, year after year, when we were all together celebrating the birth of the most wonderful legend or miracle or whatever it was, in all of Christendom. An event, an ideal, a happening that changed the world.

# Mitch Snyder
# and
# Carol Fennelly

## *SILENT NIGHT,*
## *HOLY NIGHT*

**T**HE COMMUNITY FOR CREATIVE NON-Violence (CCNV) was formed in 1970 in opposition to the war in Vietnam. We quickly came to understand that there was a domestic counterpart to the violence of Southeast Asia. For us, it was most clearly manifested in the presence of hungry and homeless people within a few blocks of the White House—the very epicenter of the Western world.

We opened a soup kitchen in 1972. Thus began our work with the homeless people in Washington, D.C. Today, literally in the shadow of the Capitol, we operate the largest shelter in the United States.

Two children in our community—seven-year-old Shamus and nine-year-old Sunshine—decided to produce a talent show as a special Christmas gift to us and the people we served. The nearly two hundred homeless people who had joined us left the hall smiling on what is unquestionably the most difficult night of the year for those who are alone.

During the auditions, the children and the adults were plagued by Lillian, a homeless, mentally disabled woman, who wanted to perform an aria from an obscure opera. Lillian is the sort who causes even the most patient and saintly servants of the poor to duck when she comes their way. She can talk faster and longer without pausing for a breath than anyone we have ever known. Because of her routinely unmanageable personality, Lillian was not given a spot in our Christmas Eve program.

A half-dozen Christmas carols had been sung, all of the gifts had been given, sandwiches had been stuffed into pockets for later consumption, and the party had come to an end.

The cleanup was nearly done, and all of our guests, save Lillian, had left. Lillian, who hadn't stopped talking since she had walked in the door, was in rare form. As usual, we ignored her, except for occasional, gentle reminders that it was time to leave.

The last mops were being swung. It had been a good day but a very long one, and we were all bone tired. As we sat quietly absorbed in our own thoughts, we hardly noticed that Lillian's chatter had ceased. It was then that we heard the music.

Lillian, seated at the piano, was playing "Silent Night"—and playing it not any which way but like a professional. Although she had told us many times of her studies at the Sorbonne and her career as a performer of note, we, of course, had never believed her.

Lillian was singing "Silent Night" in a sweet, clear voice and in flawless German. At that instant, the scruffy, loony, obstreperous old bag lady was transformed. She sat at the piano straight and proud—regal even. Lillian, in all her lunacy and brokenness, reaching deep inside herself, had offered a simple gift.

When she had finished, Lillian picked up her belongings, resumed her senseless prattle, and then walked out into the night—the night, it is said, that the angels sing.

# Robert Stack

*I* THINK CHRISTMAS REALLY WORKS WHEN you can see it through the enthusiastic, joyous eyes of children waiting for Santa Claus and all the goodies. However, as I get older, to me it becomes a time of love and sharing. For example, we have a Christmas dinner filled with not only family, but those who have no one to share it with—friends whose husbands or wives have passed away and need that reminder

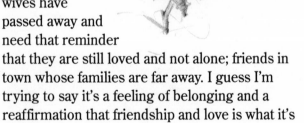

that they are still loved and not alone; friends in town whose families are far away. I guess I'm trying to say it's a feeling of belonging and a reaffirmation that friendship and love is what it's all about. Merry Christmas.

# Ringo Starr

WELL, IT WAS THE CHRISTMAS OF 1946 when I was six years old with all my fantasies intact. I was waiting at my mum's friend's house as her friend's daughter Marie was minding me. It was windy and cold outside, and of course, on reflection in every six-year-old's mind, it was snowing. It was getting later and later and I started to worry because I thought it was getting so late that Santa would pass my house by and I wouldn't get any toys for Christmas because I wasn't in bed asleep. Suddenly in comes Mum to see her little ray of sunshine with tears in his eyes crying, "It's too late, it's too late, I've missed Father Christmas." Mum, being in a happy, jovial mood, told me, "Not to worry, darling," and gave me sixpence and said we would be going home soon, which we did.

The next morning when I woke, I hadn't missed Santa after all, and my stocking was full of wonderful surprises—thank you, Santa.

# Jill St. John

## *HOLIDAY GIVING MENU*

**H**OLIDAYS ARE CONSIDERED WORLDWIDE as a time of giving. Besides material gifts, I like to give of my time and effort by preparing delicious and healthful holiday fare. An international indulgence, holiday meals traditionally bring together friends, family, and loved ones. We gather round, catch up on the latest, marvel at the way time flies, vow to see more of each other next year, and then, generally eat ourselves into a coma.

I usually spend three days preparing a holiday dinner and confess to feeling only slightly wistful when I see it consumed in fifteen minutes. I've shown my affection by going light on fats, oils, and salt. I lean heavily on veggies; as many as six are offered. I serve two different green salads, sweet potatoes, mashed potatoes, and two different stuffings for the bird. As for dessert, well, it's Christmas and all the bets are off. Margarine or butter? Herbs or salt? Turkey or ham? It's your choice. But don't forget the most important ingredient is to season it all liberally with love.

# Oliver Stone

*THE MAGIC ROOM*

**M**Y FONDEST MEMORY OF CHRISTMAS stems from my childhood in an East Side New York apartment. In those days, of course, people didn't decorate for Christmas as soon as Halloween was over as we do now. Our apartment on the East River was simply but elegantly furnished, and only the nursery had true signs of childhood life. But on Christmas Eve, everything changed, and a magical Christmas fairy visited us. No matter how I tried, I could never stay up all night long, and when I awoke on Christmas morning, the fairy had struck. There in the living room stood a magnificent Christmas tree, tall to the ceiling and loaded with colorful lights, tinsel, and gleam. My eyes would fill with wonder at how this had happened overnight. Christmas carols filled the room, and Santas and Nativity scenes graced the fireplace and tables in the room. Then I saw the presents, gay and festive at the foot of the tree. My favorite year brought a frontier fort, set up with soldiers, horses, and Indians, ready to spring to life. My heart was filled with joy and happiness at the splendor of it all.

Though I've had many lovely Christmases in my adult life—peasant cottages in rural Peru, haciendas in Mexico, beaches in Hawaii, ski chalets in Colorado—none can compare to the boyish wonder I still feel when I think of the simple pleasures my parents gave to me in that special place I called home.

# Amy Tan

## FISH CHEEKS

**I** FELL IN LOVE WITH THE MINISTER'S SON the winter I turned fourteen. He was not Chinese, but as white as Mary in the manger. For Christmas I prayed for this blond-haired boy, Robert, and a slim new American nose.

When I found out that my parents had invited the minister's family over for Christmas Eve dinner, I cried. What would Robert think of our shabby *Chinese* Christmas? What would he think of our noisy *Chinese* relatives who lacked proper American manners? What terrible disappointment would he feel upon seeing not a roast turkey and sweet potatoes but *Chinese* food?

On Christmas Eve I saw that my mother had outdone herself in creating a strange menu. She was pulling black veins out of the backs of prawns. The kitchen was littered with appalling mounds of raw food: a slimy rock cod with bulging fish eyes that pleaded not to be thrown into a pan of hot oil. Tofu, which looked like stacked wedges of rubbery white sponges. A bowl soaking dried fungus back to life. A plate of squid, their backs crisscrossed with knife markings so they resembled bicycle tires.

And then they arrived—the minister's family and all my relatives in a clamor of doorbells and rumpled Christmas packages. Robert grunted hello, and I pretended he was not worthy of existence.

Dinner threw me deeper into despair. My relatives licked the ends of their chopsticks and reached across the table, dipping them into the dozen or so plates of food. Robert and his family waited patiently for platters to be passed to them. My relatives murmured with pleasure when my mother brought out the whole steamed fish. Robert grimaced. Then my father poked his chopsticks just below the fish eye and plucked out the soft meat. "Amy, your favorite," he said, offering me the tender fish cheek. I wanted to disappear.

At the end of the meal my father leaned back and belched loudly, thanking my mother for her fine cooking. "It's a polite Chinese custom to show you are satisfied," explained my father to our astonished guests. Robert was looking down at his plate with a reddened face. The minister managed to muster up a quiet burp. I was stunned into silence for the rest of the night.

After everyone had gone, my mother said to me, "You want to be the same as American girls on the outside." She handed me an early gift. It was a miniskirt in beige tweed. "But inside you must always be Chinese. You must be proud to be different. Your only shame is to have shame."

And even though I didn't agree with her then, I knew that she understood how much I had suffered during the evening's dinner. It wasn't until many years later—long after I had gotten over my crush on Robert—that I was able to appreciate fully her lesson and the true purpose behind our particular menu. For Christmas Eve that year, she had chosen all my favorite foods.

# Elizabeth Taylor

Elizabeth Taylor, Age 12

Have a great Christmas
and everything
you want in a
brand new New Year....
all year!

Love,
Elizabeth Taylor

# Prime Minister
# Margaret Thatcher

*I* AM VERY MUCH A CHRISTMAS PERSON. The old-fashioned, traditional kind, and enjoy having the seasonal trimmings and buildup within my working environment—the Christmas cards; the Christmas trees with their lights; singing carols with my staff; and, of course, Christmas parties.

The excitement of anticipation comes from vivid childhood memories. When we would put all the decorations up in my parents' shop and I could hardly wait for all the crackers and Christmas cakes to arrive. It was a magical time.

Today I invariably spend Christmas at Chequers and always begin my day at the Christmas family service in the local church. From there I go on to enjoy a traditional lunch.

The spirit of Christmas for me has never dimmed over the years. From childhood its meaning and traditions have remained to mark a special day spent in the warm circle of family and friends.

# Lea Thompson

**I**MADE THIS HOLIDAY CARD WHEN I WAS thirteen. Then Christmas was a time for creating gifts from my own hands. My mother and sisters and I would stay up all night Christmas Eve and sew or crochet or draw. I was embarrassed sometimes by these homemade offerings, but now I think they were the best gifts I ever gave.

*Lea*

*Lea Thompson*
Age 13

# Ivana Trump

*I* HAVE FOND MEMORIES OF WHEN I was a small child growing up in Czechoslovakia and of my wonderful mother and me preparing Christmas dinner together (I was an only child and Mom and I used to and still do spend a lot of time together). Every Christmas Eve, for as long as I can remember, Mom and I prepared traditional palacinky. Palacinky can best be described as a simple, yet delicious Czech dessert crepe.

### ❧ *Palacinky* ❧
*(4–6 servings; 2 crepes per serving)*

*Ingredients:*
*2 eggs*
*pinch of salt*
*3 tablespoons of sugar*
*2 cups of milk*
*2 cups of flour*
*1/4 cup butter for pan*
*1 dollop of whipped cream*
*1/4 cup of chopped walnuts*

❧

*Method*: Beat together eggs, salt, sugar, milk, and flour until smooth. Heat a frying pan, then brush pan with butter. Pour in a thin layer of batter and spread by tilting the pan. Pancakes must be very thin. Fry on both sides to a golden brown. Spread with either strawberry or raspberry jam, roll up, and keep warm until served. Garnish with whipped cream and chopped walnuts. Accompany with a chocolate and strawberry/raspberry sauce on the side.

કર્

To this day, the palacinky tradition lives on in the Trump household. My children join me in preparing this dessert every Christmas Day, and I feel confident that the ritual will live on through the many Trump generations to come.

# Debbye Turner
## Miss America 1990

### CHRISTMAS MEMORIES

**M**Y FAVORITE CHRISTMAS MEMORIES ARE a collage of special times and traditions in the Turner house. Growing up, we had an artificial tree that came alive each year with garlands, shiny red and gold balls, tinsel, and assorted ornaments I made at school.

Every year my older sister, Suzette, my mom, and I would decorate the tree together. Then like clockwork our cats, Happy and Kitty, would try to climb,

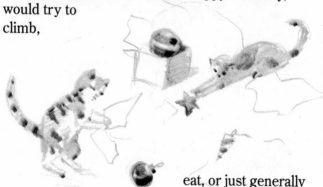

eat, or just generally destroy the tree. We have a photo of our Christmas tree falling with a helpless cat halfway up the tree hanging on for dear life.

My mom always hid our presents around

the house. I always "found" them. One Christmas morning we all (including my grandmother) had a big breakfast complete with rabbit, biscuits, gravy, and grits. Then we would clean up and go to the living room to open our gifts. Afterward, we'd all get dressed (in our new Christmas outfits), clean up the wrapping paper, and place the opened gifts back under the tree for the day's visitors to admire.

I would spend the day playing with my new dolls. Suzette spent the day sleeping. My mom spent the day cooking. And Happy and Kitty spent the day rolling and playing in all the discarded bows and ribbons.

# Robert Urich

**M**Y FONDEST MEMORY OF CHRISTMAS IS of my mom's brother Rudi. A big, rotund, jolly, if you will, man playing Santa Claus ... sitting in a circle with at least two dozen cousins being showered with lollipops and candy canes being dumped from a big, red sack.

Of course, I didn't know it was Uncle Rudi, nor did I learn until years later that his spirit of Christmas wasn't exclusively reserved for little children. That year, round Uncle Rudi visited old-age homes, hospitals, and just plain folk in the less fortunate sections of towns, bringing them good cheer and distributing the proceeds of fund-raisers, auctions, garage sales, and however else he could raise money.

I still have the suit ... his legacy continues.

# Robert J. Wagner

"WHAT REALLY REMINDS ME OF THE HOLIDAY season?"

Well, my first thought is, "Is it that time already?"

The ads are on the TV. Christmas music is playing on the car radio, and I start to think about what can I buy for ____, or did I get something for ____, or is it enough? And the whole thing starts to get crazy.

I now find myself saying—now wait a minute, is this what it is really all about? I try to focus not so much on what I am going to give to people—although that is partly what the holiday season is all about, giving someone a gift and watching the smile on his face as he opens it, the wonder in a small child's eyes as she gazes up at the Christmas tree with its lights and ornaments—but I like to reflect on the gifts that are given to all of us, such as a beautiful sunset, a clear, sunny morning, and the celebration of the renewal of life that follows the holiday season into spring. Farmers planting crops, trees blossoming, wonderful birds hatching, and the rest of nature's gifts that follow throughout the year.

This puts everything into perspective for me. The holiday season is about loving, sharing, and the expectations of things to come.

# Lawrence Welk

## A Christmas Memory

CHRISTMAS HAS ALWAYS BEEN SPECIAL TO me. I still remember, as vividly as if it were yesterday, how excited my brothers and sisters and I would be as we waited for St. Nicholas to arrive on Christmas Eve. St. Nick was really an obliging neighbor who dressed up in red robes and drove up to our North Dakota farmhouse in a sleigh, ringing a bell and shouting, "Are there any children in there?"

Well, of course we were in a fever of anticipation as we squirmed on our kitchen chairs. St. Nick would come bustling in, look at the eight of us, turn to my father, and say, "Have these children been good children all year?" After a moment of apparent doubt, Father would finally nod and smile, and we would be in a transport of delight as the good saint handed out our gifts—an apple, an orange, perhaps a pair of hand-knit mittens. Nothing expensive, that was for sure. We were a poor family in everything but love. But those small gifts meant all the world to us.

Later in the evening we bundled into the family sleigh and skimmed over the snowy roads to our parish church, Sts. Peter and Paul in Strasburg, three miles away. And that is what I remember most of all. The church was always warm, always lighted with hundreds of candles, and awash with the incense of dozens of fresh pine trees ranged around the walls. And the music was wonderful! That is not just sentimental memory on my part—our church choir was famous for miles around—and that glorious music may be what motivated me to make music my life. At any rate, it is still my warmest Christmas memory.

# Hank Williams, Jr.

CHRISTMASTIME FOR A LITTLE BOY without a dad can be a lonely time, no matter if you live in a big house with a big Christmas tree with lots of presents, like I did growing up in Nashville, Tennessee.

My father was a star. Not just a twinkle, but the biggest star in country music; the first star in the Hall of Fame; the first star to have pop recording artists record his songs, "Jambalaya," "I'm So Lonesome I Could Cry," and the list goes on and on.

His name was Hank Williams and I'm his only son, "Bocephus" Randall Hank Williams, Jr. He left me when I was three. I remember, faintly, my dad, and a Shetland pony he gave me for Christmas. The pony was placed with me in my dad's limousine...that's why I remember. The horse was kickin' and he was trying to calm me and the horse down.

So, as a boy, my mother gave me big, exciting, and empty Christmases. Really, the one Christmas that turns a warm spot on in my heart is the memory of a one-eyed granddad taking his grandson rabbit hunting on Christmas Day. That ol' man, my grandpa Sheppard, didn't have a house as big as mine in Nashville, but a small place in the Enon community of lower Alabama. His wide place in the road was the North Pole with all the reindeer (except they were cows) to me. You know, as I think back on that Alabama Christmas scene, now I can see the twinkle in Granddad's good eye as we ate the rabbit I shot for Christmas Day. Merry Christmas.

# Michael Winner

**M**UMSIE ALWAYS LOST A LOT OF EXTRA money at Christmas. She'd get excited by the gala dinner and the fireworks at Cannes Casino and rush off to the gaming room. To celebrate she'd play at four roulette tables at the same time. I can still see her, an elegantly dressed, lovely, white-haired, tiny lady, pushing through the Christmas throng to place her bets—usually on zero or a combination of zero and one—laughing when she won, and making a minor expletive of horror when she lost.

Over a period of about ten years from 1970, Mumsie lost some five million dollars at the Cannes Casino. They liked her there quite a lot. And in spite of her losses, she liked them, too.

Unfortunately for me, to pay her gaming debts she'd set off in a taxi the next day, the back stuffed with paintings, jade, and other antiques, all left to me by my father, and sell them at local shops around the south of France.

She finally sold the apartment, which was also left to me, and ended up in a small room at the Carlton Hotel. But she'd had a helluva time getting there!

She's passed on now to the great roulette wheel in the sky. I don't know if they have Christmas galas up there, but they *must* have a bit of gambling to liven things up, don't you think?

"Zero-one," I can hear her calling out to the angel in charge as she hands him her chips to put on the green baize. I'm sure you can't lose up there. Now that really is heavenly for her.

# Jonathan Winters

### *A Little Boy's Christmas List*

I SURE HOPE WE HAVE ANOTHER BIG Christmas tree with all the lights and stuff on it. And my stocking—I hope it has a little more in it, last year it was only half full. Every year I ask Santa for a train, but I never get one; that book on trains Uncle Ray gave me isn't the same.

I hope Aunt Lou doesn't give me another scarf. The guys always say it looks like a girl's. I'd sure like a *Star Wars* costume, but Wally, the kid up the block, said they were all bought up before Thanksgiving.

I asked Santa in my letter if he'd make Grandpa well enough to come downstairs for Christmas Eve. I wonder sometimes the way the mails are if my letter really gets to the North Pole. I seem to be the only one in the house that writes to Santa. Santa, if you hear me, could you find it in your heart to give me a real good set of earplugs. I just can't stand to hear Sis's rock albums any longer.

Oh, by the way, Santa, would you send me Mr. Robert's book, *Math Can Be Fun?* I really don't want it (I hate math), but now that I'm in the third grade I'm desperate.

I also need a new fishing reel, Santa. The old one's okay, understand, but Dad says next spring if everything goes okay, just him and me are going way up to Canada, where the big ones are, so I don't want to take a chance of losin' that big one.

Santa, do you ever give those big silver dollars Grandpa used to get? If it's worn, I don't care. I know Dad carries one for good luck. I'd put mine in a secret hiding place.

You know something also I'd like, Santa? It isn't necessary, but I could do with a new pair of mittens, sheepskin lined. My wool ones are shot. They don't have to be expensive, just real warm!

Santa, I know I'm not allowed to come downstairs on Christmas Eve when you fill the stockings, but would you do me one small favor and let me hear your sleigh when you take off from the roof? My room is way at the other end of the house, so you gotta ring 'em real loud!

Santa, I realize you've got so many things to think about, and so much to deliver to kids all over the world, but you know the two things I would settle for more than anything? That every poor kid gets a wonderful toy—one that no one else has—and a wonderful Christmas dinner. And I know you'll laugh at this, but you know what I really want from Dad? I want for him to pick me up, kiss me, and tell me he loves me. (Mom does it, but I guess Dad forgets!)

Santa, before I forget it, I'm gonna make you a promise, one that goes for you, too, Mrs. Santa Claus, and all the elves: I'll cut my list down to just five things. Oh, and by the way, if you should give me that fishing reel, I'm sure Dad would let you go along with us to Canada to go fishing. Besides, I'd really like to get to know you, when you're not working. You know kids all over the world love you. By the way, how do you go around the world in one night?

# David Wolper

*I*N 1939, I SAW TELEVISION FOR THE FIRST time at the 1939 World's Fair and fell in love with it.

From the time I saw that television set in 1939, all I wanted in my home was a television set. In 1944, my father finally decided to buy one. This set was gigantic, the screen was no more than eight inches across. We used to have to watch with a magnifying glass in front of it. But that memory of my first television set of Christmas 1944 is one that will stick with me forever.

It will stick with me forever because it brought something even more important for Christmas than my getting the set. My grandfather was ninety-six years old. For whatever reason, I will never know, I just wanted him to see television before he passed away. He had seen the coming of the telephone, the electric light, the automobile, the airplane, and radio. The relatives brought him over to the house so he could see television. He passed away two years later. Little did I know that television would be my life's work...or somehow maybe I did.

# Michael York

**H**OLIDAYS ARE TIMES THAT SHOULD IDEALLY be spent with family, renewing and strengthening ties. Due to the rootless, peripatetic nature of my job, my definition of "family" has to be extended to include a larger kinship of professional associates, especially when working abroad and away from so-called "home."

One of my favorite memories is of Christmas spent in the deep south of Morocco in a little desert town called Erfoud, on the edge of the vast Sahara. I was making a French film and the entire crew was *en famille* in a hotel where the road stopped and endless sands began. We ransacked the local stores for gifts and exchanged them with as much pleasure as if they had been Cartier bijoux. We danced whirlingly to jolly accordion music, and Jojo, the genial special-effects wizard, made the night vivid with his fiery skills. But perhaps it was the star-filled sky over the cold desert, the palm trees, and the mud buildings that housed people clad in costumes unchanged for thousands of years that reminded me of traditional Christmas cards and their depiction of that significant nativity that half of the world now celebrates as a holiday. It was a land where camels and donkeys were still used for transport, and

where stables and mangers were still essential.
I remember being very grateful for my room
at the inn.